MW01249297

WANPIS

WANPIS

RUSSELL SOABA

Port Moresby
**University of Papua New Guinea Press and Bookshop
in association with The Anuki Country Press**
2012

University of Papua New Guinea Press and Bookshop
P.O. Box 413,
University PO, NCD,
Papua New Guinea
Phone: 326 7375 or 326 7284
Fax: 326 7368
Email: upngbooks@gmail.com
www.pngbuai.com/buybooks
in association with The Anuki Country Press

WANPIS
© 2006, Russell Soaba
ISBN 978 9980 869 59 3 (HB)
      978 9980 945 22 8 (PB)
Reprint 2012
First Published in 1977 by
The Institute of Papua New Guinea Studies, Port Moresby
in conjunction with Kristen Press, Madang.

All rights are reserved.
This publication is copyright. Other than for the purposes of and subject to the
conditions prescribed under the Copyright Act, no part of it may in any form or
by any means (electronic, mechanical, microcopying, photocopying, recording
or otherwise) be reproduced, stored in a retrieval system or transmitted without
prior written permission. Inquiries should be addressed to the publishers.

Printed in India by Sterling Publishers Private Limited, New Delhi-110 020.

I

LUSMAN

I lay on my back, legs spread, silently observing. My roomate had warned me numerous times not to. But I had rather liked it. Observing the picture of a near nude dim dim which was stuck directly above the foot of my bed, I mean.

"That girl is white," said my roommate and pointed to the picture while sitting at the edge of his bed. "But-awa kotena-" he then added— "do I like her. Tell you what, I wouldn't mind..."

I wasn't listening then. Or at least I pretended not to.

I thought I knew my roommate well just as he thought he knew me. Just Call Me Joe was what he called himself. He preferred that name which he adapted from a Western film he saw somewhere to his Christian name. I too, had, in protest, erased my names in my birth certificate. We wanted to be independent. As far as I knew Just Call Me Joe, he was the usual happy-go-lucky, easy-to-get-along-with Papuan, always eager and willing to conform to anyone's disposition just for the sake of laughter. And all he believed he knew about me was that I was "a quiet but brainy little village idiot". We'd decided not to go beyond that. If we did we'd start crying then.

"Hey mate," said my roommate after a while of silence, "know something?"

I did not respond. I was watching the picture. The near nude dim dim made me think of Enita.

"Mate," quietly repeated Just Call Me Joe, "I'm talking to you."

"What? I returned without much thought.

"Know what happened last night?"

I did not answer.

"Something happened last night," Just Call Me Joe kept tugging at my senses.

"What is it?" I then asked, more uneasily than reluctantly, sensing that he was about to make his usual jokes on me about the night before. "What happened las night?" "Nothing. Ha ha." He then mumbled something aloud which escaped my ears then threw himself on his bed, imitating me.

"No seriously," he sighed a little later, "I reckon we are nothing."

"How do you mean..."

"Well , just get up and take a look at your small face in the mirror. You know what you will see?" He paused, looked at me for a moment then said, "Nating ia."

"What are you getting at?" I said, raising my voice a little.

"There," Just Call Me Joe shouted, pointing to the mirror of our room. "You have a good look at your small self in that, mate. Hell, did you realized we both haven't had our ears pierced."

"What?" I jumped off the bed and looked at myself in the mirror. My ears weren't pierced. Which meant that I had not been initiated in the village.

Just Call Me Joe rose from the bed and we both paced the floor of the room. We each completed a couple of little circles in our pacing, without words.

Suddenly Just Call Me Joe laughed. It was a bitter laugh. He began pacing the room more restlessly than ever. He swore, he kicked at the chair, made a few holes in our room by breaking two or three louvers, and then punched a large one on our hard wooden door. Passerby showed faces of amazement through the holes then strolled on after shrugging their shoulders or suggesting we both should report ourselves to the Warden of Students for damaging the University property. Or, to make things easier for everybody else, take a walk to the Laloki Psychiatric Centre. But my roommate just laughed aloud and told them between numerous four-letter words to mind their own affairs.

We left the silent room to the near nude *dim dim* and went outside. Dusk was here. The sun was burning low in the west, behind the near-silhouetted outlines of the Main Lecture Theatre and the adjoining administrative buildings. The sky, with little dots of dark purplish clouds, which looked like black clay pots placed over a slow flaming fire, was red. Like a mud-smeared, fly-swarming tropical ulcer. The overall atmosphere of that dusk, then, resembled a weird monster that stared at us through blood-shot eyes. There was nothing romantic about that dusk. Except that I, the *lusman*, loved it.

"Now what's so special about dusks?" asked my roommate when I stopped by the door, gazing mutely to the west.

"Nothing much," I remember sighing, "except that it was on a dusk like this that I was born. And I spent the first moments of my life in the darkness, waiting for dawn."

"You poor *lusman*," he exclaimed sympathetically. "You poor, village, idiot bastard."

And Just Call Me Joe laughed. Almost guffawing.

That's how Just Call Me Joe and I were. Our conversations began with lust and ended up meaningless with the dying dusk of each day. Often we talked a lot, using a lot of words, sometimes big English words too, about nothing. We were students.

Yet however meaningless our words sounded they had always contained in them, we felt, little bits of truth which we could only wonder if they had found their marks in the people we used to direct them to. Even now, while lazily looking out through the louvers of a Government-rented house at the northern end of Port Moresby city where I am writing this, pretending I am doing it to please myself or to let the thought of a dying friend out of my mind, I can only wonder if those words we used to say at Uni. meant anything to anybody at all. I wonder if the children playing *kung fu* just outside the house know anything. I even wonder if the people of this country know what I am all about.

But, to make a mild confession, I have said, without opening my mouth, a lot of things which saddened the hearts of my elders like Father Jefferson and Mr. Golds-worth. And even Just Call Me Joe himself. For instance, I had assumed myself to be far more traditional than my Papua New Guinean colleagues. Naturally, I was fearful about this. So I withdrew from everyone else. My wife wasn't amused. It was her presence, I think, that made me realize the urgency to save my being, my soul, from no one else but me, and my fears soon turned out to be something akin to fatal menaces against my desire to be happy, to remain alive as well as sane within my chosen surroundings.

I was born at dusk. True. I spent the first moments of my life in the darkness, waiting for the next dawn. True again. Symbolically, that is. I never did, and perhaps I never will, know what that next dawn was. Still, I strived to find it one day, somewhere.

There is no doubt that first sixteen or seventeen years of my life were spent in the darkness of common humanity—callowness, simplicity—and of blind conformity to a new world which I could not totally understand. Yet I was enthusiastic about this new world that became the environment in which I grew up. Civilization, as it is sometimes called. Even Father George W. Jefferson, the respected Principal of my old school, was pleased about my enthusiasm when I went to see him in his office-and-residence one evening. This was in mid-November of my final year at high school. The other school leavers had already been similarly interviewed by the Principal.

It wasn't much of a building—the Principal's office-and-residence, I mean. The old man fancied bush materials, native carvings of primitive patterns and expressions ranging from oral myths and legends to the recent historical events (mainly displays from one end of the office to the other of wooden-carved portraits of the early missionaries from the first day of their arrival in this country to their sorrowful martyrdom in the last war), and tapa cloth curtains for the house. All, except the corrugated iron roof, were of native outlook. It was indeed an improvisation of a haus tambaran. And out of that modest building came the myths and legends of my country, together with the necessary splendour, richness and love of the Christian teachings.

"Come in!"

It was the Principal who called. I heard him before I had lifted my hand to knock on the door which was open.

"Come in," Father Jefferson called again.

I tucked in my shirt, straightened my collar, brushed the tangled mess of my overgrown hair with my palms then walked in.

"Ah, it's the Deputy Head Prefect himself!" The Principal exhaled a sigh of satisfaction.

As well as being the Deputy Head Prefect I was one of the outstanding School Certificate students that year.

"How are you?" asked the Principal, addressing me by my Christian name.

"Quite well, thank you, Father," I answered.

"Well now," said the old man, clapping his short hands with excitement and sounding less formal than I had usually known him to be, "let's see, ah...er...yes..." His fat fingers moved through the pile of folders on his desk, all employing a certain kind of rhythm of movement which only a pianist could identify and perhaps name, looking for my records. The face of the old man reddened a little, not out of sudden exhilaration or the contrary, but because of the dying sun that flooded its weak rays through the half-opened window. There was no hair on the old man's head. A sign of dedication. In most parts of the country baldheads arc highly respected for prominence of prestige as well as some numerous traditional prerogatives in the village community. Some students at the school had joked at one stage that the old man shaved that head when no one was looking. But this was real. Dedication. The lines of the dewlaps directly beneath the chin darkened, and the throat turned blue due to his morning's lack of shave.

"Ah, here we are," sighed the Principal when he had found a folder with my name on it. He read out all my names aloud then looked at me and smiled. "Obviously there is no criticism at all I can think of," he said without having opened the folder and smiled again. "Well done, son." Then another long, exhilarated smile followed and he said, "That's all."

I turned to leave.

"Oh, one moment."

"Yes, Father?"

"You know the history of All Saints' pretty well, don't you?"

"Yes, Father."

The Principal rose from his chair of canes and ambled over to the picture frame directly opposite his study table. He looked old; limbs were about to be cramped; every movement of the old man was indicative of lethargy caused by hard work; life, it seemed, was gradually ebbing from him. He eyed the picture of a young man, presumably in his thirties, cleanly shaven and in an army uniform—an RAAF flying officer from World War II—for a long time. Father Jefferson then let his eyes wander slowly away from the picture to his own shoes, then across the wooden floor and up to my face. His gaze remained frozen on my face.

"You do remember him, don't you?" the Principal asked, referring to the picture of the young man.

"Yes, Father," I answered. "I know him well." He let his stare fall from my face. "And Father," I added a while later, "I am thankful. Very thankful."

"I am glad to hear you say that, my son," he said, then remained silent as if he had forgotten what he was to say next. But then he spoke again, at the same instant the dinner bell began pealing down at the Mess. I remembered that it was my turn to say Grace before the meal. "You do know, of course, that without him we all wouldn't be here," was what he said in a far-off tone.

"Yes, Father."

"There is also a possibility of him—" and with the word 'him' the Principal pointed to the picture of the young man—"coming up to the Territory on an official appointment, mainly within the Administration; and the chances are that you might meet him in person. In fact I do recommend that you must. But he's a careful man, a busy man, in which case every possible chance of even inviting him here for All Saints' Day celebrations will be very narrow indeed." Father Jefferson paused for breath then added, "But the chances are obvious. You might get yourself acquainted with him."

"Father?".

"You might get to know him more in person. In fact, I do recommend that you must."

"Yes, Father."

"He's a wonderful man, a great man."

"Yes, Father."

"And remember, my lad: we owe him all."

"Yes, Father."

"Very well then. Just remember that, wherever you are destined to be."

"Yes, Father."

A moment of silence followed. I swallowed my saliva.

"That is all, son. You can go now."

"Thank you, Father."

I turned and walked to the door. I remembered that the dinner bell had been rung ten or so minutes ago; All Saints' students were waiting for me to say the Grace.

"Oh, one last thing," I heard the old man's voice when I had reached the last of the steps to his house.

"Yes, Father?"

I re-entered the office-and-residence to find the old man's back turned on me. He was a troubled man, I could clearly see.

"I am satisfied," he sighed at length, without turning to me. "I am quite satisfied with our conversation this evening, my son."

"Yes, Father," I responded.

I took a final glance at the picture of the young man on the wall, at the traditional carvings, then at the young man again.

Under the frame that supported the picture of the young man were some beautiful writing which read: "Flight Lieutenant Archiebald William Goldsworth – Founder of All Saints'."

All Saints', in the years that I knew it, stood like a township but more like a district Mission station in the silence of its atmosphere, down in a valley and walled in by several hills. The school was about a mile from the coast and had been blessed with an airstrip cleared by the earlier students who were then men enrolled for the first time at a school atmosphere, a power house,   • six modern constructed and bush material classrooms—the latter being wall-less and allocated to the junior forms—and twelve half-Western, half-tradilional buildings that accommodated the staff and students, including Father Jefferson's office-and-residence. The sea was about a mile from us, and its vast expanse of deep blue could conspicuously be viewed from the tops of the hills that surrounded our school. No one had the thought of even commenting on its presence, however. Only once had one student, Jimi Damebo or James St. Nativeson as he was known to us, who had possessed incredible talents in creative writing, written a lament about it;

> O sea of solitude
> whenever will I
> embrace your serenity?

And that seemed to be all. At the weekends the best the staff and students could do was run up to the hills of Taworakawa and Rewai, which rose immediately after the school grounds and seemingly turned their backs on the sea, to watch over the tranquility of the valley wherein lay the school, motionless. From the top of those two hills the choice was an individual landscape viewer's: it was either All Saints' in the valley below or the wide 'sea of solitude' in the opposite direction. The plan for the positioning and erections of the buildings was symbolically legendary and traditional: a cross laid down in the centre of the valley. At the head of the cross stood Father Jefferson's office-and-residence, followed by the houses of the staff and the Chapel which was the centre of all buildings: the six classrooms stood meekly on either side of the Chapel after which was the Mess and finally the dormitories which completed the rest of the body of the cross. Succeeding the body or foot of the cross was the playing field which was green and very quiet Once. I imagined, trees stood there, near which wallabies drowsed lazily in the happy sun. Village hunters stalked those wallabies, and through the skill and craftsmanship of those times forgotten many had died for supper. There may have been tribal feuds on that field, where probably the blood of a certain chieftain had spilt so that the victory and glory went to another tribe which was now anonymous. The chieftain too, whose blood had leaked into the soil of that field, was anonymous. Now, no one from those old days lived in that field and the nearest village was miles down the coast. The field was therefore deserted, but on which All Saints' students occasionally played games, cackled and giggled, ate and lived. Just after the playing field was the airstrip, lying in wait opposite Taworakawa and Rewai hills and outstretching its arms to meet the sky that brought in its planes from outside. Further beyond was the brief gully for the planes to land and lake off, the tropical virgin jungle and the rivers that never ran dry. Rainy seasons were common and agricultural projects formed by different Science Student Clubs brought the school her diet of *kau kau*, German and local taro, bananas, yams and peanuts; there were four poultry farms, a hundred goats and five steers with several cows to give protein to our elders, and to us on All Saints' Day or whenever there was surplus. The whole valley was rich, content.

In All Saints' itself everything was green and silent. Students and teachers entered a classroom with a certain objective or dedication and that look of dedication on their faces was also conspicuous in the Chapel, in the dormitories, at work, every-where. Everyone, including Father Jefferson, knew and felt that he was a very special person, a saint. At the beginning of my final year at All Saints' I was asked by the Principal to escort a couple from outside to the hills of Taworakawa and Rewai. The couple scanned the valley from one end to the other and sighed with satisfaction. In the end the wife exclaimed:

"Darling, isn't it beautiful. So idyllic, so tranquil."

"It is rather too quiet," was the husband's reply.

"But I love it that way."

"It's too quiet," insisted the husband, in a tone of uneasiness. The woman turned and eyed her husband. Her face was flushed and the gap between her eyebrows formed two vertical wrinkles. Then the wrinkles disappeared.

"Darling?" she was now saying, calmly, and from the corner of my eye I saw her hand reach out for his. She withdrew it.

The husband turned to me: "Do you like your school?" he asked.

"Yes, Sir. I do like the school."

"I still say it's too quiet," the husband decided, in a tone of firmness, his face abruptly averted from both his wife and me. The man's words sank into the valley below like a piece of lead thrown into the depths of a dark ocean.

There was no ricochet.

In the following days after that interview with the Principal I carried out my duties as the Deputy Head Prefect for All Saints'. Father Jefferson, our Math, Science, English and History Masters including our Head Prefect were away at the time at an end-of-year teachers' conference in Soya Pier, and were expected back by the end of that week with a fresh supply of Bibles for those of us who were leaving. Before leaving for Soya Pier Father Jefferson had chosen James St. Nativeson, two other prefects and me to help our English and Math teachers, the only lady teachers at the school, tutor the juniors with their homework.

The most the other Form 4 students could do, now that the final exams had come and gone, was to await the Principal's return and as well keep watch over their little brothers and cousins in the junior forms to finish off the final term. After which the whole of the student population would disperse in all directions, throughout the country.

Late after dinner on an evening of that week I was on my way to the junior dormitories to round up the little ones to their classrooms when a boy called from the door of a senior dormitory. The young Form 4 student was calling and beckoning me desperately. Before walking towards him I turned and called two small boys, who were twins, chattering noisily in Motu in front of the junior dormitories.

"Blake, Byron. Get the others to your classrooms before Sisters Margaret and Susan wring your necks. Quickly, quickly. It's already half-past six. And don't ever speak in your native tongue again, unless it's a weekend."

"Yes ia, Brother Prefect," the twins resounded my voice in the quiet of the evening then darted into their dormitories. Within seconds there was a timid hubbub of hurrying little figures towards the classrooms, some boys slapping their exercise books noisily against their bodies, others clawing at their oversized shorts which were slipping from their waists, several complaining of lost rulers and pencils, one shrill voice within a dormitory calling out insults at the senior students for a stolen rubber then three or four late ones jumping out of their abodes to make last minute dashes or steal nervous glances in my direction before slowing down to easy strides.

"Come on, hurry on there, William and Napoleon," I shouted after them. But as if in answer to my shout a lone junior shot out suddenly from the now vacated dormitories and, making the very last minute dash after the others, cried, "You seniors stole my rubber. I will report you to Sister Margaret. Thieves. Robbers. Primitives."

To this there came a collective hoarse reply from the senior dormitories composed of obscenities, careless grammar and fabled promises of violence. But the junior was safely out of sight.

Silence was retrieved in All Saints'.

"Brother Prefect, in here," the boy from the senior dormitory resumed shouting. "In here." I walked towards him. "*Weu*, my brother," he said helplessly as I got near. "It's Just Call Me Joe again."

•

"Why, what has he done?" I asked, brushing past him.

I entered the dormitory to be confronted by a row of cane beds on which some boys stood, some sat, gazing at me with stunned, mouth-opened faces. The whole room was filled with silence and stares. Just Call Me Joe was among the faces and he was the only one in the room who smiled. He was standing on his bed, hands by his hips and towering the others who were smaller than he. I turned on the light and sat at the edge of the Head Prefect's bed. Then, aware of the stares, I jumped down to the floor of the dormitory.

"Well, what's the matter, Nathaniel?" I turned and asked the boy who had summoned me.

"It's J.C.M. Joe again, brother," answered one of the boys on behalf of the shocked Nathaniel. "He kissed the picture of the Blessed Virgin."

"What's wrong with that?" laughed Just Call Me Joe.

"She's our Lord's Mother," I heard the stunned Nathaniel speaking out for himself behind me.

"She was Jesus Christ's mother," said Just Call Me Joe.

"She is our Lord's Mother," cried young Nathaniel almost shrieking. "She's no ordinary woman..."

"I know she's no ordinary woman," retorted J.C.M. Joe.

"She is no ordinary woman to be kissed like that—I mean, to kiss Her picture like that," said Nathaniel.

"So what?" returned J.C.M. Joe. "Bring all the virgins of the world and I will show them..."

"Stop it. Stop blaspheming, Joseph," said the other. "You just got St Joseph's name for nothing."

"Ha. *Aio Mamo*," laughed J.C.M. Joe wickedly.

"But why did you?" Nathaniel kept saying. "It's an unforgivable sin if you kiss our Lord's Mother like that, you know that."

"I only kissed the picture," J.C.M. Joe defended himself.

"The Catholics kiss the Holy Mother," someone joined in the argument, not knowing whose side he was on.

I looked out into the dark through the windows, wondering if the other prefects and Sisters Margaret and Susan could hear the noise and the argument. For the moment the boys were lucky Father Jefferson had taken almost all the harsh teachers to that conference in Soya Pier.

"Of course it is one of the Catholic customs to kiss the Holy Mother," the same boy repeated.

"Well, brother?" Nathaniel turned to me. He looked at me straight in the eyes. "Well, brother? Aren't you going to report the matter to Father Jefferson when he comes back? You... you are the Deputy Head Prefect... and a Christian... aren't you?" He stared directly at my face and added, "He showed no respect and fear towards our Holy Mother."

"Yes, Nathaniel," I told him. "I am the Deputy Head Prefect. And a Christian."

Moonlight flooded the valley of All Saints'. The juniors were silently doing their homework in their wall-less classrooms as I walked past. Occasionally two or three coughed, but all had their heads buried in their books. In a few years' time, Father Jefferson had once explained to me, the school would find enough money to build better and permanent classrooms for these little students. Already in Australia Mr.Goldsworth was doing all he could to have the necessary funds raised.

An owl hooted in the dark parts of the bushes that surrounded the junior classrooms. Some of the students looked around them, but after being sure that it was only an owl resumed concentration on their studies. I walked on. In a Form 2 classroom I saw Sister Susan peering over the shoulders of one of her students to help him solve a problem.

I ran up the hills of Taworakawa and Rewai to watch the silvery gray tranquility of the school below. The lights in all the buildings were on and the crucifix became a living glory of fluorescence under the moonlight. Behind me the moon itself rose higher, and as I scanned the heavenly serenity of the valley, it wriggled its way up the clean sky until it was directly above me. Assuming Sisters Margaret and Susan wouldn't notice my short period of absence I decided to brood away for sometime. In fourteen days, I realized, I would be leaving All Saints', and that made me feel glad. Just Call Me Joe, James St. Nativeson, Nathaniel and others would also be leaving. I wondered if there was anything in All Saints' that I would regret walking out on. I could distinctly sense then that being glad of walking out of the school was simply a feeling which I would grow out of one day, somewhere. But at that moment, while sitting and viewing the valley, while wondering if it was Just Call Me Joe who should be put on detention or Nathaniel to be comforted with the suggestion that the argument over the Holy Virgin was only natural and human unless one was completely possessed by the devil, I was glad I was leaving All Saints' at last, perhaps for no other reason than to grow up, to change.

Someone whistled at the foot of the hills and I realized the other Form 4 students were about. I stood up, stretched and yawned. I looked up to the nocturnal sky which was romantically clear with the light of the moon. The air was cool and fresh with the falling dew. And the overall atmosphere was just as bright. Like dawn. The whistling from the foot of the hills came again, closer this time. Remembering Sisters Margaret and Susan, I stole away from the whistling and crawled crabwise down the hill until the silence of All Saints' swallowed me up.

"Is that you?'

"Yes, Sister Susan," I replied.

"Oh good. Good. Listen, Sister Margaret has a headache so could you and Jimi round up the Form 2s and Form Is? It's fifteen minutes to nine."

"Certainly, Sister Susan."

'Ta so much. And good night."

"Good night, Sister Susan."

I walked towards the junior classrooms. From the last unwalled classroom, where the boys from the dormitory I temporarily took charge of were studying, I heard low, well-controlled murmurs and giggles. I hurried on to investigate. I was almost taken aback when I discovered from a short distance that the class had got itself into a small cluster right in the middle of the room, with all the boys peering into the centre of the circle they each constituted. From the middle of the pack I could hear one of them, reading a book to his classmates who listened attentively, sighing "Iaa, brother, read some more..." and clawing into each other's ribs between well-controlled convulsions of short giggles. None of them was aware of my presence.

"William," I shouted at the reader.

The small cluster of bodies scattered, like an hibiscus flower being spun and torn to shreds, petal by petal, since the designers of our school uniform had chosen the colours pink for our shirts and green for our shorts. The boys panicked, some of them bumping into me in their mad rush to get back to their desks.

"On your feet, William," I heard myself roar. "Hands by your side, eyes to the board and keep still."

The others froze in front of their desks. I walked up to the front of the classroom until I was facing William. He was trembling while trying to hide the book behind his back.

"Keep still."

He too froze.

Extending my hand towards him I said, "I shall have that book, William."

He handed me the book. I flipped through the pages. A James Bond series. "Where did you get this book, William?"

"From Prefect Jimi Damebo, Brother."

"Did he recommend it to you?" No answer. "I asked, did he tell you this was a good book for you to read?"

"No, Brother Prefect."

"You know you are not allowed to read dirty books."

"Yes, Brother..."

"Did you ask James to give you this book?"

"No."

"So the book walked away by itself and found itself in your hands, eh?"

At this the others laughed. I was sure they would. William's face became distorted, after which tears began streaming down his cheeks. The others stopped giggling.

"I did not ask you to cry, William," I said. "In this school we are no longer small boys. We were men from the very first day we walked into All Saints'. And our parents are too far away for us to..."

A hand shot up from a boy sitting next to William.

"Yes, Napoleon."

"We are men, Brother Prefect..."

"That's what I was just telling you," I returned irritably.

Napoleon ignored me and rose to his feet.

"Therefore," he went on, "we do what men do. So I am going to tell you this like a man, and you can punch me on the head if you want to, Brother Prefect. It was not William who got the book from Prefect Jimi. I asked Prefect Jimi Damebo to give us the book because he told us there was a story about a very intelligent English spy..."

"...who came to All Saints' in the guise of Napoleon who is now asking me to include his name for detention next Saturday," I finished the sentence for him.

"Yes," Napoleon raised his voice a little, both with contempt and a sudden stare of surprise. Then anger showed on his face; two little balls of fists began to take shape by his hips.

"All right, big boy. Tell us what you think."

"Brother Prefect," Napoleon began, his eyes fixed on the board and without any emphasis to his voice, "Sister Margaret told us to read as many books as we can, to broaden our knowledge. Whether they are good or bad, we should read them all so that when we leave this school we will be better off. You see, it is useless just reading one kind of book only. We should read others as well, so that we can learn not only to enjoy them but criticise and question them as well. After all, we are trying to get ourselves educated, aren't we?" For a moment I couldn't believe it was a junior student speaking to me, least of all a Papuan christened as Napoleon. "Brother Prefect, we should learn to allow ourselves to know everything," he spoke on, this time allowing anger and frustration more than anything else well up in his voice. He then looked at me hard and said, "How much have you read, Brother Prefect?"

I did not answer. Only stared back at him in disbelief. William stopped the flow of tears from his eyes but was having difficulty in knowing whom to fear; to him it was either Napoleon or me.

"Well, Brother Prefect," Napoleon sighed with scorn, "seeing that you are one of the brainiest students in All Saints', I hope you don't end up being a writer, because... because how can you fool the world when you haven't read enough? Like some of these Papua New Guineans who think they can write poems and short stories in English."

"Did Sister Margaret tell you all this, Napoleon?"

"Yes, of course. And Prefect Jimi too. They told us we should learn to be aware of everything through reading. And Sister Margaret told us we should learn to be independent, to think for ourselves, and speak for ourselves."

No wonder Sister Margaret doesn't get far in All Saints', I thought.

"Also," said Napoleon, "Prefect Jimi told us that if we want to improve our understanding of the world outside this silent valley we must do a lot of reading. That's our only choice."

"On books like these?" I held up the James Bond in front of him.

"On books written with a touch of logic in them—if we know what logic is."

"That is what Sister Margaret and Prefect Jim think," I said testily. "But what do you yourself think. Napoleon?"

"That is your problem, Brother Prefect."

He sat down. He then motioned William to sit down without my consent. The others murmured inaudibly but kept silent instantly afterwards.

Outside the nine o'clock bell began pealing echoingly through the moonlit serenity of the valley.

"All right, friends," I said, clapping my hands, "time to move." The little ones rose, carefully packed their exercise and text books, pens and rulers, after which we formed a line and marched to their dormitory. For the remaining two weeks of my final year I was in charge of these little ones, the lowest junior class whose prefect had left soon after the final exams, because of "family problems'". The Form 4s I had been residing with had no need of a prefect since we all were, by this time, regarded as ex-All Saints' students.

I switched on the light and while the boys got settled or started tucking themselves into their cane beds, I ran over to Jimi Damebo's dormitory to return him the book. Jimi was in charge of a form 2 dormitory. He was brighter than most of us, and had been excelling tremendously in English and Creative Writing since coming to All Saints'. He read widely and as a result had christened himself James St. Nativeson after owning two or three copies of James Baldwin's books. We weren't allowed to read Baldwin's novels (there weren't any in the school library, anyway), but St. Nativeson had managed to have them smuggled into All Saints' through his girlfriend at Soya Pier High School. The girlfriend, Vera Nonda'isiri, was a frequenter of Port Moresby city, especially during school term holidays, and that was probably how the books found their way to Soya Pier and finally to All Saints'. When I entered his dormitory James St. Nativeson was trying to monopolise the one light to read a thick book while his boys quietly chatted among themselves.

"May I see you outside please, James?" I said.

"Oh," he said, looking up from the book. "Yes, do - at your service, Deputy." He threw the book on his bed and came away. Over his shoulder he told his boys to stop talking while he talked with me outside.

"Ia, that one our Deputy Head Prefect," exclaimed a boy who sat up on his bed and waved to me.

"Maybe Brother Jimi is in trouble, ah?" said a boy near him.

"I said, no more noise—Oscar, Terence," Jimi Damebo shouted at the two. "And speak better English than that, for goodness sake. Really, Napoleon and others are better off than you lot."

"Yessa, Mr Prefect Englishman," returned one of them.

"Ia, du not moeda da Kwin's mada taangh," laughed the other.

"Lon lib awa nobol Kuin," chanted the rest down the rows of beds.

"Da liwa Jordan is lunning wely lafidly."

"Da Mista Bonaga vas feeping thlough da vindow to see vat is haffened."

"Aiya, my blada, da bus is came, da bus is came..."

"Ah, stoffit, yu poorish figs," shouted a very small boy from the far end of the room. "Shaddaff or I lefort yu to Susa Margaretta."

There was laughter from every corner of the room and James shrugged, like a rebel.

"Ladies and Gentlemen," someone quoted in an attempted deep voice, "this is the BBC in London. Let us all be perfect Englishmen. And speaking like a perfect Englishman, allow me to assure you that the weather shall be fine..,"

"All right, all right, cut that out," shouted James St. Nativeson. "Really, you are..."

"Ei, brothers," interrupted a small boy nearby, "and about Aussies, how they speak English? Ia, how, how?"

"A wouldn't 'ave a clue, mite," said James and grabbed the inquisitor by the ears. "Now if ya don't do as y'r bloody told, I'll tear y'r ears ta pieces." He then pushed the junior onto his bed and we left the dormitory.

From outside we heard the small boy yell, "Ah, pissoff, ya black pommie." James, rather than agitated, turned to me in the moonlight and smiled with content. He said, "Those boys learn fast, don't they? They know about the world outside this valley more than any other class, don't you agree so?"

"Yes," I said, "when they are children their minds are fresh." With those words I gave him the book.

"Now whose side are you on?"

I told him I was on my side.

"I don't see why they shouldn't read these books though," he tried to argue as we moved away from the dormitory to the dark shadows provided by the short coconut trees, at least to be free of any junior overhearing us.

"We are not totally preventing them, Damebo," I reasoned with him. "Besides, it's useless asking or even expecting these kids to be mature men overnight. They have yet to acquire the right state of mind to decide between right and wrong. They need time to mature, Jimi. For the moment they are just too young..."

"And underdeveloped and innocent? Brother, you are worse than some of these fools who attempt to hide all kinds of perversity by being nothing else but moralists, moralists, moralists..." He paused to cough vigorously then muttered, "Morons." He turned his face away from me. Pressing his head onto his chest, he shook it frantically. Without turning to me he went on, "They are quite definitely going to reach the age of maturity, these boys; there is no stopping, no waiting, nor even growing back. You should know that, brother. A fellow with brains like you should, surely."

Then turning abruptly to me he said, "At least that is my concern. That is all I have to be proud of: knowing it as a factual truth, then telling it to the world. Wanting, in fact, dreaming, to become a writer one day, is to somehow give voice to this silent valley, to expose it to the critical scrutiny of the world outside. Hell, brother, how else must we be liberated? Frankly, don't you feel bored being here?"

I assured him I understood his arguments, but to become a writer, as James well showed the potential, one shouldn't do so as a means to release one's problems upon the world; or shouldn't attempt to turn the world upside down or something of that nature which I had read in a book somewhere.

"A simple thought," sneered James, but his voice was calm. "A simple Christian sentiment of be-kind-to-your-neighbours. What matters is to dawn on light on both sides, if you know what I mean." The moon hid its light from him. "But believe what you will, brother," he spoke on, "and whatever it is must be solid. Stand firm on it and fight for it. And I hope you don't end up being like me. People like us die like frogs on the road." He paused to cough vigorously again. It was the result of excessive cigarette smoking, one of the school rules that he, Just Call Me Joe and others were keen on breaking. "You know," he then said, "this may sound ridiculous to you but after having read some heavy books I seem to be sure of my destiny or at least have some ideas about it. And that destiny is, as Just Call Me Joe would put it, nothing but my own fault; self-neglect, as others would put it; which all boils down to the fact that I am a Papuan who is too young and has no authority, no rights whatsoever to the language that I speak now, which is hard - if I want to become a writer. I even hear some teachers say, "No, you cannot become a writer unless you have done this and that - unless you are recognized as so and so because your reader will expect these of you. Which is true to a degree, but I am desperate to become a writer and that's what makes them stop and stare at me; desperation, that's my problem, a lusman's problem. So being such a lusman, all I have left is my tradition, its values and demands, plus my soul, and my dreams—rootless dreams, if you like." He paused again, then leisurely began kicking the grass beneath him.

I said nothing.

Jimi Damebo took a deep breath, then sighed: "You know, I sometimes wish I could go to a high school in Australia or somewhere abroad—I don't say this out of prejudice, no, no, I hope not; I say this out of some urgent psychological necessity, if you know what I mean... at least to go to a high school where I could think and write freely, read whatever I wished... and above all, to step outside myself and feel the free air, to explore that sky up there, the universe, after which I could weigh out my own condition, or at least have an attempt at understanding it..."

The moon completely hid its radiance from us. In that darkness, James stopped speaking, as if my silence meant that he had said something wrong or that he had said all this because of my presence; and as if to conceal that 'guilt' further, he asked, from the dark: "And why didn't you go to other high schools like in Port Moresby or even in Australia? You are the only one here..."

I wanted to explain as I did so many times to him, to Just Call Me Joe and others that I was a Papuan, born in the village, as much as they, but dismissed the desire for just the reason that even in repeating the remark about such an individual as well as natural right I could be lying both to James St. Nativeson and myself.

> One day unique children will be born
> to tell us all, "We would like for you
> to know you owe us a little something",
> with I the conserved captive.

The lights in my 'transit' dormitory were still on when I returned. The boys were either asleep or pretentiously snoring away. At the far end of the rows of beds, however, two little voices were singing, like a pair of doves cooing:

> *Madi bema gabu daudauai*
> *be do baina hereva henimu...*

The noisy twins, I thought; afraid of speaking in their native tongue again have now decided to get away with a local song.

"Blake, Byron."

"Yes, Brother Prefect?"

"Shut your mouths and get to bed. *Haraga!*"

"Oio.. .sorry, yes, Brother..."

"And say your prayers before doing so."

"Yes, Brother Prefect." After a few moments of silent whisperings at the sides of their beds, the twins hurriedly tucked themselves into their torn, gray blankets and called, "Good night, Brother Prefect. God bless you, brother."

"Night," I returned, thinking, "I have no brothers."

The last of the fourteen days stalked, crept over the hills of Taworakawa and Rewai and walked over All Saints' with its late November morning sun to startle most Form 4 graduates who were asleep and dreaming within the indifferent tranquility of the crucifix. In a moment sunlight flooded the valley, revealing the mucous blue of smoky mists and heavily fallen dew along and on top of the dark green hills that caved us in or walled us, as if in protection, against the sea. Only the junior students, together with those members of staff who would remain in the school for some time, embraced that morning with mild if not numbed innocence. The other students like Just Call Me Joe and James St. Nativeson had only to anticipate seeing this day which marked the end of a dark night and the beginning of a new life.

In the Chapel, during the Mass for those of us who were leaving, the boys sang the farewell hymn with a unique sense of sorrow. In one part of the Chapel a few boys wailed aloud, thus creating a rather flat but harmonious melody to the tune Sister Susan was playing on the piano. They wept because this was a time when they were to go out and face the wicked world—the new challenge—armed with the Bible and Father Jefferson's blessing; this was a time when self-reliance was first felt; a time when they were to shape and polish their characters and possibly become leaders of their new country. They would never again see Father Jefferson, their best friends with whom they had shared everything, good and bad; above all, they were losing all the refuge and confidence that they had depended on for four years. Few were willing to leave All Saints'.

After the Holy Communion we were presented with our Bibles and the Farewell Mass came to an end.

Yes, it was the end of the term at All Saints': the end of our adolescence the hardest part was yet to come - initiation to manhood.

And now, after we had ourselves comfortably loaded on the school's utility, on top of piles and piles of our luggage and food and ready to leave, what was there in All Saints' that I should regret walking out on but to join the others view a few things we would never see or chat about again: the few coconut trees, the dormitories, the crucifix, the playing field, the airstrip, Father Jefferson and Sisters Margaret and Susan. Blake, Byron, William and Napoleon, led by Just Call Me Joe, James and Nathaniel, ran forward and shook my hands, wishing me all the luck there was in the world. Blake and Byron, through tears, assured me with their *bamahuta*, *kaka* that they would pray for me.

"I have no brothers", I reminded myself and smiled faintly at the twins. The utility jerked into motion, hastened to its restricted speed of twenty miles per hour and we were off on the coastal road to Soya Pier where we were to catch the Mission boat, *Quartz*, and sail south for home. *Quartz*, after dropping us at the appropriate ports along the southeastern coast, would then return to Soya Pier for the next lot of student travelers in the opposite direction. Just Call Me Joe, James and others would be on that trip. Blake and Byron, William and Napoleon, had three more years left before they could see home again; or if their parents were able they would see home every year. Nathaniel was traveling to Port Moresby through Soya Pier to start immediate employment because of 'family problems'. Those from the immediate localities had already begun walking, their packs on their backs, and in all the four directions away from the valley.

I looked back at All Saints' now disappearing behind the hills of Taworakawa and Rewai. The corrugated iron-roofed buildings with their *kipa* walls and supported by hard *bendoro* posts became smaller as we weaved our way along the sides of the hills towards the coast. From the top of a higher hill the overall view of the school below became a mixture of brown and silver crucifix, laid down in a quiet but rich and fertile, green valley. The utility glided down the slope of the last hill and that was the last I saw of the school.

Miles of dusty dirt road took us further southward along the coast and past villages whose names we had never been told before but which we understood to be the squalor-stricken dwellings that were yet to be civilized. There were fourteen or so such villages, remotely distanced from each other by about six or seven miles, and linked by the only dusty road from All Saints' to Soya Pier. The road meant little or nothing to these villagers and its only purpose to them was to begin at All Saints' and end at Soya Pier. Later we stopped at a village which I had known very well by sight and location, especially through my previous Christmas holiday journeys to Soya Pier in search of casual employment. The village was just as anonymous as the rest and as yet no one had attempted asking further for its name or even giving it one. Whether the villagers were reticent in giving us the name, or not much anthropological research had been done in the area, one could never be sure. Only once had our History Master at All Saints' tentatively adopted a name for the village in an article he had sent to *The Current Condition of the Pacific Ocean,* but external scholars and critics immediately dismissed the suggestion as "mere guess work". Since then the village just remained the village, and the area that surrounded it was generally regarded as the 'Goldsworth District'. Having stopped at this village the driver of our utility asked the villagers for some coconut milk for us. A minute later the headman of the village came to our service. He was kind enough to let his people climb the only coconut tree there was, which stood meekly at the centre of the village and which barely had enough green nuts left. In exchange to this we offered the villagers some tinned meat that we carried with us for the journey. The headman, after nods of approval from the other villagers, refused our offer with a smile.

"Omui maragidia be All Saints' taudia, ah?" the headman then asked.

"Oi be," we chorused, simultaneously translating the elder's question to our juniors as "He said, 'you small ones are from All Saints', ah?"

"Yes ia," echoed the juniors.

We cut open the green nuts and as we drank the milk, the headman said, "It is good to see you young ones from school. You are doing good for our name. We are proud of you." The elder was addressing the skies, where what he saw was clean emptiness.

The sky was just blue, cloudless. Like human innocence and wholeness, left untouched. I realised then that the people of that village were brutally cursed by the dry season. It seemed they had not seen a day of rain during all that time that we were at All Saints'. The trees that provided the only shade for the village were devoid of living green and the surrounding landscape looked far from the enchantment one expects in the tropics. Children with prominent outlines of ribs about their bellies swarmed around us, noisily sniffing thick layers of mucous; but their attention was drawn more towards the utility than to us. Two or three of them walked up to the utility and timidly touched it.

"It's surprising how we are what, forty miles from All Saints? - yet we see nothing but dryness," said a senior student.

"Yes," said another, "I wonder why All Saints' is so rich with fertile land and yet this village suffers."

"It's because the school's situated near the mouths of big rivers, you idiot," returned his senior counterpart. "Shit, how come you are still dumb after getting good marks in Geography."

"You are going home for holidays?" the headman asked.

"Yes," we all answered.

"Your parents must be glad to see you back."

"Yes."

Just then a youth brought us some more green coconuts, placed them carefully at our feet, straightened himself up nicely, then grinned. I noticed the lone coconut tree was completely stripped of mature green nuts.

"Oh, this is my little boy," said the elder, pointing to the youth. "I was trying to send him to All Saints' last year but the school fees are too high."

"He looks stupid," a senior student, the Geography student's counterpart, gurgled the words through his coconut milk.

"Yes," continued the elder in Motu, "it was too much for me to send the boy to high school..."

The headman paused. The driver of the utility winced. Time was running out and the driver had to return to All Saints' either by midnight or the early hours of dawn after dropping us at Soya Pier.

Nevertheless the elder continued, "But it is good to see you young ones of education. Some day you will show us a lot of things we don't understand."

The driver restlessly thanked the village elder and rapidly yapped orders at us to board the utility. We did. Before getting into his seat the driver paused, then ordered me down.

"Quick, quick, Brother Prefect," he spoke rapidly. "You tell for first years what for that cement in middle of the village. O.K., quick."

"Oh."

I jumped down from the utility and cleared my throat. As the others watched and listened I explained the mystery of the cement block that jutted out of the middle of the village, near the lone coconut tree.

"That is the Goldsworth Memorial," I told the juniors. "You know that picture of the man in a flying officer's uniform we see in Father Jefferson's office.'"

"Yes ia, Brother Prefect."

"Well, this is where he was shot down by the Japanese."

"*Aia Mamo,*" they returned sadly.

"And when he was shot down the people of this village found him and nursed his wounds until the Australians and Americans came and got him out."

"Teh, tch, tch, tch," the small ones marveled, shaking their heads in wonder.

"We know about this Memorial but it's too far for us to come down from All Saints' and see it," said one junior. "Maybe if we have excursions every year to this place is all right, ah?" The senior students just watched and employed pretentious yawns.

"And brother?" asked another junior.

"Yes?"

"How come we are situated far from this Memorial?"

"I don't know," was the only answer I could give the boy since the driver was becoming impatient again.

We drove on through the dry land, the Goldsworth District. Patches of black were splashed against the brownish hills where there had been *kunai* fires, and the shrubbery around the area put on the color of reddish olive and general lifelessness. Goldsworth almost died for us in this part of the country. And on our left, along the beach, were the wrecks from the last war. On All Saints' Day we remembered the war and how so many of our elders have died for us by the samurai slices and butchers of the Japanese soldiers.

By nightfall we were at Soya Pier. It did not take us long to unload our luggage and food from the utility and re-load them onto *Quartz* which was all set and ready for our arrival at the pier. We thanked the driver and watched him drive off into the night.

One of the boys asked the Captain for the time of the boat's departure and when the fat and sleek-haired gentleman grunted 'twelve o'clock sharp, but make sure you're not left behind' the seniors were off. And they would not be back until a short while before the boat's departure. Usually they went to the Soya Pier surroundings and by luck acquainted themselves with the nurses or the girls from Soya Pier High, telling them they were from All Saints' and wondering if perhaps a little walk along the beach mightn't be such a bad idea after all...

The juniors and I took advantage of their absence and asked one of the crewmen if we could use his saucepan to cook our dinner. The Captain overhearing our request, offered us a huge billycan with some trimmings of a yellow fin tuna they had caught that morning.

"And after you have had your dinner," said the Captain, "you can sleep in the *dim dim* passengers' cabin. There should be four beds vacant there. You can all fit in. And forget about those big boys. They can sleep anywhere on the boat."

"Thank you, Captain," we said.

We did our cooking upon the shore, just beside the pier. Over the flaming fire and the boiling pot the juniors sang some Church chorals and hymns or talked generally of their homes, their parents and relations.

We had our dinner then later the Captain announced that it was midnight. We journeyed on.

How right James St Nativeson was when he said that there was no 'growing back' for anyone; that once one walked out of a place there was no room for a return. Leaving All Saints' was just as sad, as desolate as being released from prison or walking out of a home. There must always be another place to go to. And the 'crime' in all this, as he had once put it, is when one has no choice: when education is no longer an excuse: when one has to keep on going, to 'die like frogs on the road' - or die an 'alien death'. After which; what would Jimi Damebo suggest?

> But I shall return to tradition
> When I have died me that alien death;
> And for our reunion I'll bark you
> A lap lap of tapa designs and cry:
> *Oro da! Oro kaiva!*

Or simply a dream, a fruitless nostalgia?

Yet I have learnt a lot from James. I learnt for instance, that there had been a crime done on my life. Crime in the sense that I was born without choice, like a random bearing from a machine that had finally fallen out of place. Or, as I learnt from a book which he had lent me, I was a man without a beginning nor an end. Those students at All Saints' were right when they used to describe me as 'the boy who has just appeared here'. And as James himself, out of his excessive unconventional readings, had once put it: it's horrifying being a man without a home, without a soul; as if your parents had preached and lived a certain humanity, without you.

At the same time I had no one in particular to blame for such a misfortune, except myself. The other students thought that way too. But they, such as the juniors who were traveling with us, saw and knew the word 'home' more than I because they could always go back to their villages and look up to someone they could call mother or father ('Mother, I have come' or 'Father, I am home') and be rewarded with the emotion that they were thought and taken care of whereas I, no matter how hard I strived to conform to their world through long moments of strenuous imagination, could not. All that I could now treasure was the understanding that I was sixteen, undersized, and that I had left a village which should be my home, I believe, at seven, to go to the islands for my primary school then to All Saints' for four years.

"You did not sleep at all."

It was the Captain speaking behind me. He did not see me attempt a smile, while sitting hidden from the cabin lights, the way I communicated at times.

"You did not sleep at all, small boy," he repeated, probably wondering why I didn't answer him.

"No," I said.

And the Captain laughed. Carelessly.

"You seem so different from the other boys," he then said.

"Different?"

"Well," said the Captain, sounding ponderous, "you don't seem to be in their group -I mean, you don't seem to..."

"I don't mix with them easily."

"Ah, that's it, that's it."

Someone in the cabin (he must have been a crewman experiencing some dream) shouted loudly, and later made short, jerky cries of relief, like a wild animal blurting out victorious wails during some ecstasy of a sort.

"Dawn's breaking," the Captain interpreted the man's dream.

"Yes," I said. "Dawn is breaking."

"You must be excited about going home," said the Captain.

"I don't know."

"You don't know?"

"I don't know."

The sky in the east was gradually beginning to brighten, becoming a little yellowish, but all the time endeavoring to retain its vast mass of dark olive, like the skies I used to know at dusk. In it remained silence: a long moment of dark silence - not to mention the noise the engine was making and *Quartz's* slicing of the wide, semi-darkened Pacific with her prolonged sighs. The short cries from the man in the cabin could be heard no more. Soon a light brush of grayish blue swept across the horizon before us, to let us know we were sailing into dawn.

"How long you been away?" the Captain asked after some time.

"Been away?"

"From home."

"Oh. Nine years."

"Nine years?"

"Nine years."

"You must be excited about.... going home then."

"I don't know."

Minutes later the sun showed itself a little above the horizon, a red semi-circle behind the morning clouds of dark purple which in turn gradually became baked to the color of burnt sienna, then later into a heart-warming purplish gold. The breeze that came to us from the sunrise was cool, and could well console a troubled soul by its morning freshness.

The gentle ripples from the surface of the sea which repeatedly reflected little stars of gold rose to meet the rising sun in eager embrace. Not far from *Quartz*, and just a little to the south of us, was the land with its vast spread of obliterated mangrove green and dark olive hills that were slowly being transformed to goldish brown by the sun's rays. Watching every little phase of that sunrise and its effects on the waiting dark earth reminded me of a place I once saw, still too young but old enough to memorize. Yet to name or define that place I found it impossible.

"It must be lonely being away for a long time," the Captain spoke again, slowly, as if transcribing my thoughts. 'You must have been a little boy when you left home?"

"Yes."

The tone in my voice made him swerve suddenly, as if he wanted to make sure he had asked a fair enough question. I noticed that the Captain was observing me through narrowed eyes, now that it was light enough, and in the same way Father Jefferson and Sister Susan had once done and asked who exactly my surname belonged to.

"And your father is a business man?" the Captain asked at last, in a way a hunter grabs a wallaby by the tail. "Or a coastal trader? A plantation owner?

"I have never known him," I answered.

"Oh, I am sorry."

I noticed a faint but knowing smile form across his face, though he looked away immediately to avoid my stare of "Don't worry, Captain. It's good to see one express an opinion." He, however, comfortably decided to keep the conversation, flowing. "Don't worry," he said lightheartedly, "you got all the education in the world to be free of the past."

Laughing carelessly, he changed the subject.

"Would you believe me," he now said, "if I told you that there is a place beyond that sun that is rising over there? And that I come from there?"

"I think I would," I answered. "In fact I do."

The Captain let out another short and careless laugh, this time as if sure of the fact that I was only pretending to know what he was talking about.

"But it's simple," I exclaimed, trying to prove my capacity for deep thought.

"I am glad you believe me, young man," he could now speak at ease. "Let me tell you something that is very tricky, but most fascinating, if you give it a careful thought. See, beyond that sunrise, let's say over six thousand miles from here, there is another place, a land perhaps, perhaps an island, or even a big country, where the shadows of her men are slowly, slowly growing taller, just to merge with each other until they disappear completely into the darkness. Whereas here, still the same distance away, our shadows are slowly, slowly beginning to grow shorter."

"It is dawn to us," I said.

"And sunset to them," he echoed.

"Then it will be sunset to us."

"And to them also the dawn."

"But the sun just remains."

"And the ocean lies free, motionless."

"With the shadows jumping to and fro, changing places, all the time."

The Captain gazed towards the east, a smile of sudden happiness forming across his face against the light of the reddish ball before us.

"Which do you think is safer?" he then asked. "The sun or the ocean?"

"Why, the ocean, of course," I returned. "The sun burns. I'd much rather spend the rest of my life in this Pacific Ocean because it somehow makes you feel something."

"It does. It does."

The Captain fished out a packet of cigarettes from his hip pocket, took out a box of matches from his breast pocket and played with the two little things with his fingers, deep in thought. Then, taking a cigarette from the packet, he said, "You see, this spread of the wide Pacific is only a replacement of a place where you would want to be. There is no blood, no flesh, in it; it just lies there, motionless, immortal—in fact, a kind of immortality that has no sentiment of the everlasting mortality of man." He stopped to place the cigarette between his lips. "It is merely a thought, a dream, but at least you would kind of feel free," he continued, "with nothing before you for miles and miles around. Know what I mean?"

"Keep speaking, please," I said, deeply interested. He lit the cigarette. "It would be very lonely for you," he went on, "with your feeling at times that you were a prisoner, your own prisoner —if you know what I mean."

"But it would be better that way. And anyhow, I was born of it."

"Ah yes, I understand what you mean. And better for everyone else because—" he paused to turn to me—"because this would be the only time and place for you in the world, where you could get closer to one thing and one only that man strives for."

"And what is that?" I asked, so desperate to know.

"Contentment," he said simply.

"Contentment?"

"Yes. Complete human contentment. Completely complete. After which, of course, come in things like peace, peace of mind, human understanding, love, creation of new worlds, even greed, avarice..."

"And greed and avarice are always there," I interrupted in anger.

"Quite," agreed the Captain calmly, which made me feel that I had no right at all to be angry, especially on my own behalf.

The Captain spoke on: "Unless—unless, of course, one is prepared to retain that contentment by simply responding to the changing times with one's sensitive creations, rather than letting time itself feel imprisoned by one."

"But before reaching that contentment, life is nothing but a wide sea of solitude," I offered, remembering James St. Nativeson.

"Ah yes, my young friend. Our sea of solitude."

There was a far away look in the Captain's eyes when he had said this. The cigarette which was barely puffed down to the butt had disappeared mysteriously from his fingers, possibly forced out of his grip by so much discontent that brewed deep inside me. Then as if inevitably, he concluded, "Which is why I left my own country. Behind that sunrise."

We stopped there, to let the cool morning breeze absorb us completely, in which time I had wondered how on earth this Captain, this complete stranger, a Polynesian in fact, had come to befriend me. What is it, I asked myself, that is so fascinating about human beings when two complete strangers meet at a certain place, at a certain time, at a certain span of their lives, just to feel and understand a thought they had suddenly discovered to be their common meaning which in turn enabled them to consciously know for the first time that they had in fact unconsciously been knowing each other for a long time? It reminded me of a book I had borrowed from Jimi Damebo in which two original yet unpublished writers, a Frenchman and an Englishman, both of them sharing the common philosophical thoughts in the one and only poem each had written, without having met each other in any way whatsoever, until quite by chance, upon one cold winter in Paris, when both rush to the nearest bar to weep away their defiance at the world that is so blind and silently oppressive.

O Vera, Vera Nonda'isiri,
why pour your heart upon my soul?
There have been men, poets, already
in existence and full, so full, of the sea.

The crewmen and the other All Saints' boys, or 'Sainties' as we called ourselves, awoke to greet the morning sun. Two or three staggered sleepily towards each edge of the boat to pee over the rails. They had slept well, I noticed.

"What time will we be at Posa Bay?" I asked the Captain.

"Nine o'clock tonight," he answered.

"We'll be sailing a long way, Captain."

"You will need some sleep then," grunted the Polynesian as if I had just asked for a favor. "It will be a long journey yet, First Mate," he added amicably, as he moved off to chat or exchange schoolboy jokes with the other Sainties.

There is nothing much to know, to add, to one's life and history. One is born to be oneself: to live, to die; to have everything; to have nothing. Home, therefore, is a personal reference—of birth, of language, of the sense of belonging and possibly necessary symbolism—before death. That ambushed my mind; I was afraid of the soil on which I stood. The other Sainties must have noticed my indecision, since they were scrutinizing my being against the brownish semi-barren landscape. But they waved to me with the Captain; only uncertainly.

One of the smaller boys was kind and sociable enough to call out both my Christian and surname. Then later, "Brother, good luck."

"Good luck, Brother Prefect," the others joined in vaguely.

One of them called out loudly: "So long, Brother Prefect. You double-skin, fadah-less, pretentious basta."

I swung my pack over my shoulder and turned away. A few steps later I turned to steal the last glance at *Quartz*. She remained motionless against the wharf as if still asleep from the previous day's journey from Soya Pier. At noon she would sail further south, across the sea to the islands, to drop the other boys. The Captain waved to me.

I ran up the rocky path, walked past the Posa Bay Patrol Post Office, ignored the road to the airstrip and chose the bush track that ran north and later westward along the coast.

The sun was high already; ready to burn the trees, the grass, the earth, and me. It was going to be a long walk, and twenty-six miles of it. I endeavored then to convince myself I was going home. I tried picturing the village I saw nine years ago. There were ten houses; a few coconut trees behind each, some more still which spread to the beach, and a giant mango tree in the middle of the village. The mango tree towered above a house which belonged to Enita and Mary. And the people? Only a few left. Anyone would guess that, since death was part of the village atmosphere. As well as that many had left for towns and cities and the few who remained used their absence as an excuse to lose hope. Malaria consumed much of their hopes and prayers for survival. And Enita? I could just remember her face, no more, and distinctly. And Mary? She was ten when I last saw her; a skinny long-legged girl, screaming at me to shut my eyes before tearing off her *pumapuma* to swim in the sea.

Continuous, uncertain walk took me through a countryside of savannah, only too equatorial at places, across dried up streams and riverbeds and over numerous low hills. I was beginning to recognize the soil on which I was born. This was the Anuki district. James St. Nativeson had once been to this part of the country and had described it as 'another way of looking at the Goldsworth District'.

There were several geographical reformations I could not remember seeing before. Some parts of the long road had either been moved to the left or right. The dry riverbeds too must have just been born. Home, I knew, was miles in front of me. And far behind me was Posa Bay. But at that moment there was nothing in front of me, or at the back of me. Only the road, the low olive shrubbery, and obliterated reminiscences based on a seven-year old boy's memories.

Hours after the sun had bent its midday knee I was within the boundaries of home. Some Anuki people claim that they can walk from Posa Bay to Yaguyawa-Kuburina in half a day. Others say less than that. It took me a whole day to do it, and it was already dusk when I arrived.

From the top of a nearby hill I saw the village. There were not ten houses. The giant mango tree rose from the middle of the village to meet the sky, with the old house being overtopped by it. It must have been pruned while I was away, not by people but by time and anonymity. The house too must have been rebuilt. Enita, I thought, had grown old; so the Yaguyawa-Kuburina villagers had probably decided that a little house would do for her and Mary.

Seeing the village after nine years renewed that sense of belonging in me. I let out a shout of joy and ran down the hill, slipping at places, my pack half-flying on my back, and forgetting all the pains I had earned during the twenty-six-mile walk.

A young woman stood in my path at a distance of fifty yards or so when I neared the village. She must have been on her way to urinate when she saw me, and stopped, to let me pass perhaps. It was getting dark already so I could not make out who the woman was. So I smiled. She didn't. But the face caused me to hesitate before walking on. No, I thought, she can't be Mary. My face must have worried her because she too stopped and stared.

"Wasina?" I greeted her.

"Tam aiyabo?" she responded.

"Me," I answered and read out my Christian and surname.

I read out my names again, this time adding Enita's surname.

"?"

I thought I saw a slight expression of surprise on the woman's face. She probably didn't expect me to speak the Anuki language, or probably thought that the way I mentioned my names was sadly funny. She turned and walked away, apparently postponing her desire of urinating or relieving herself otherwise. I followed her. She was wearing an old grey dress, long, crumpled, and her feet merged and melted with it in the fog of the evening light. She appeared as if she was floating in the wind just above the ground and towards the village. Out of some urgent emotion, completely controlled by instinct, my internal restlessness compelled me to call out after her.

"Mary."

The woman stopped without looking back.

"Mary?"

She walked on.

"Mary. It's me."

She still walked on, half-running. I must have changed a lot in nine years, so she couldn't recognize me.

"Mary," I kept calling, "remember me?"

She ran on. There was a lot of clumsiness in the way she climbed the steps of the little house under the mango tree. Then she disappeared into the dark rooms within.

I stood in front of the house, shocked. Somehow I had managed to gain enough courage to keep calling to a woman who was my sister, who hid herself away from me and in our house.

"Mary," I called. "Don't you want to believe me? I'm your brother. I swear it. I swear I'm not..."

While I raved on in complete madness a very small flock of children, speechless men and women, gathered around me. Some smiled, others looked me over in utter amazement; the older ones came forward and held my hands with their faces turned away, while two or three stood and watched from a fair distance. A youth of my age, with whom I might have played years ago, with whom I might have shared the usual sins of childhood, walked up to me, shook my hand, called my name, amicably called me *bariyawa* and my nicknames which I could not remember, said I was a big boy, then strolled off... I then discovered that I had been, in fact, shouting at Mary in English all that time.

I slipped off the pack from my back and, with feelings of guilt and desolation all mixed to form a spinning well of confusion in me, climbed the steps of the house. The atmosphere of the interior was cool (the fire places not being used for days, I guessed) and the rooms were dark. From the corner of one room came short, successive and jerky gasps of uncontrollable sobbing and wailing.

"Mary?"

There was no answer; only the sobbing and wailing and some vigorous shaking of a small, dark heap of Mary in the corner.

"Mary, *bada Enita meme?*" I asked, this time in Anuki. "Where is Enita?"

To answer my question, Mary leapt from the corner, blanketed me into her womanly body and, calling out my Christian name repeatedly, cried like a child.

"You are going away."

I did not respond. I just stared. Absent-mindedly and at the sago thatched ceiling above me.

"You are going away again," quietly repeated Mary, as if I had not heard her. "That's what those papers mean."

"I know, Mary," I said, in the same tone of voice as her's.

Three letters lay open on the bed near me. One, a letter of congratulations from Father Jefferson about my success in the School Certificate examinations, the other, of approval from the Dean of Students to enter the University of Papua New Guinea's Preliminary Year, and the last, a sincere word or two from my scholarship officials advising me to collect my travel warrant at Posa Bay for the journey to Port Moresby.

All the three letters were two weeks late in reaching me, or in reminding me to leave Yaguyawa-Kuburina again.

"Must you go away?" winced Mary.

"I must," I said, without further thought. "I must, Mary."

An inevitable outburst escaped her: "Sinda oh," she cried. "You been away for long time, I always want you home for long time but you never come. And now you going away again. Why, why must you? Look at me. Like I'm growing old and useless, ah? And the house. It's growing old. And the gardens. They are growing old too. And the land..."

Mary, in her weeping, repeatedly told me of the land I was born in, the land that remained quiet and forgotten since the beginning of time. To Mary, as much as any Anuki villager, the land had its own story: of the winds that came and went and no one knew the direction from which they came and to what destination they were flowing. The outside world was like the wind. And the wind was their favorite folk tale or legend. They knew nothing of it; they expected nothing from it. They had no desire in knowing about it; they had no desire in rejecting it. They just felt it blowing, blowing. Whatever the wind had done to the land, whether for good or for worse, the people witnessed it, memorized it, did not mind it. And talked about it, as a myth. There were talks of cyclones blowing houses down and uprooting trees; of the tides rising every year and the land sinking. The people felt no anger or remorse. It was an invisible wind, anyway. Listening to Mary all that afternoon, I felt guilty of being part of that wind; guilty of coming to the village with it, then disappearing again with it; guilty of brushing off my own sister's arguments, as if she was an old rag, a mere pebble of clay, forever dissolving into time, into the abyss of nothingness. And I imagined it all; the day of my departure, I mean. Mary crying under the mango tree with one hand holding mine and the other covering her face, pleading that I must remain with her till the end; Sinada's dead, she is reminding me of Enita; and it was not her fault that she wasn't allowed to marry in the Church after having two children out of wedlock; I know we have different fathers, brother, but she was our only mother; it was she who bore you, who breast-fed you, who called you a son, who gave you a home, gave you your beginnings, gave you the blood of the people you are walking out on...

"Surely", Mary was now addressing me through tears," we must matter. Remember, you are the boy out of the two of us, and we can't just end now; we can't just be the fatherless children, or bastards as some people call us. We've got to begin, got to begin now. We are people, human beings, the same as the others. And our past is the same as theirs; which is a long, long story of this land on which you stand and say you are home and call yourself *Anuki*, and own it more in words than you actually know about it". She shrugged helplessly and stared at me in dismay. "No," she said with another shrug, "you will never understand because you are not a man yet. And you'll never be. And when you are away", she went on grumbling, "will you think of me? Ah? Mary? Mary. What does that name mean to you? Nothing. Like those other people who go away, and are too busy eating Europeans' dung they forget their own people. No, you won't think of me, brother. I can see that in your eyes. You are laughing at me. You been away for long time and you never understand this place; because I'm crying for something you don't recognize..."

She stopped abruptly and sat beside me, weeping quietly. She looked sad and far away. Too far away for me. A tired old woman, at nineteen.

"And two of us our future, how, how?" she startled me with her quiet voice, after a moment of silent weeping. "Eh? You tell me brother, how?"

"Nothing," she answered herself. "Nothing but dead silence."

She turned away, biting a lip in deep thought. Then slowly she controlled herself. She had reached a decision. To be alone once again.

"Think you will find him?' she now calmly asked, without looking at me.

"Find him?"

"Father," she said. She turned to me then running her fingers through my hair, added, "Your father."

There are many people in the world; it's no use walking up to a total stranger who bears the same surname and saying to him, "Hullo, Dadi." Turning to Mary, I shrugged, "What's the use? I'm a *lusman.*"

I met Just Call Me Joe at the campus and learnt a lot about the University, the people, and the city through him. Mr. Archiebald William Goldsworth, J.C.M. Joe informed me, was already in the country and he, Just Call Me Joe, had had the first privilege of meeting the founder 'in person'.

"We must meet him again some time," he said excitedly.

He took me down to the dormitory where he had claimed a room for us. The room was bare; a few posters, probably left by the previous occupants, including a color blow-up of Che, hung along the walls beside our beds. Che was on my side of the room and I promised myself to read about him later during the semester. A photo of a near nude *dimdim* hung directly above the foot of my bed. She smiled as I made my bed with the sheets Just Call Me Joe had obtained for me.

"Want to tear her down?" J.C.M. Joe asked of the near nude.

"No," I said, thinking of Enita. "Leave her".

I finished making my bed and sat on it testily. I had never slept on a mattress before. J.C.M. Joe had indeed prepared everything for us while waiting for me to catch up with him at the campus. My study desk was already packed with biros, pencils, a ruler, exercise books, some folders and several writing pads. We had no curtains, two study chairs, a mirror, some emptiness and silence for the room.

The silence hung in the air around us, in which J.C.M. Joe fished out a crumpled cigarette from his hip pocket. He lit it and smoked the silence up. Fumes, stranded, sailed unresistingly around the room.

"Relatives at home," he asked at length, "are they well?"

"Sister is."

"Oh?"

"Enita's dead."

"I'm sorry."

"You needn't be."

"You mean, you didn't know all that time we were at All Saints'?"

"No."

"Not until you got home."

I nodded, then lay on my back, legs spread...

"Man, you really were moping all through the holidays, all right," said J.C.M. Joe. He laughed carelessly then spoke again with deliberate care, as if cracking some philosophical joke of the day, "I can read your mind, brother; lucidly. You really have reasons enough to start hating some people now." He lay back on his bed, studying the near nude. A while later he said, "No, seriously, brother, I am sorry. Very sorry."

"You needn't be," I said.

It was the orientation week, explained Just Call Me Joe, "the idea is to get ourselves acquainted with our new environment." We were standing outside our room, facing the Main Lecture Theatre and the administration block which were on our left and the Arts/Law building which was almost to our right. The idea of setting up a Student Village was not thought of then, so what we saw on our right was a brief bitumen road which just scratched past the Arts/Law building and was immediately linked up by a dusty track that ran through a semi-olive Moresby bush to a new suburb, almost completely hidden from our view, called Gerehu. Further to our right were tropical gum trees, sparsely distributed, and swampy benoguga grass patches that weren't at all green. That side of the campus almost reminded me of the Anuki district. Yet directly beneath us was a small resort of rich green modestly shaded by a couple of young rain trees, and since it was only the 'orientation week' I decided not to let it remind me of All Saints'. I noticed that the sun was sailing towards the hills far behind the Main Lecture Theatre which meant that the western sky was on our left, where the sunsets would be. On our right was the east, although it would mean my waking up early enough to rush out of the room, turn right, then walk along that floor of rooms to the end of the building from where I could catch the sun.

"By the way," said Just Call Me Joe, "the name of our dormitory is Tuloan; that's 'friend' in a Bougainvillian dialect, I think."

We spent the rest of the afternoon exploring the campus. It was too early for studies, although quite a number of students walked past us with thick books under their arms, expensive fountain pens jutting out from breast pockets and comics resting academically among the texts. J.C.M. Joe was waving to or exchanging enthusiastic smiles with them, some of whom stared at me. I then wondered what it would be like for me to be carrying piles of books around the campus for the next four or five years to which my disposition had forced me to assign my miserable, naked self.

We saw a lot more students; most of them appeared in colourful floral or posh Western dress; others, like J.C.M. Joe and myself, wore faded blue jeans or inferior looking grey shorts and random or All Saints' T-shirts. I had the temptation to assume that there were two groups of people at the campus (and possibly more); the decent and careless ones. I had difficulty in deciding what group to conform to, or in what group I would know that I was myself and not somebody else. But of course at All Saints' life had been easier.

Just Call Me Joe had briefed me about various student organisations at the campus: there were political movements formed by the students; one was allowed, he told me, a choice of different clubs such as religious, cultural and other studentship activities which catered for individual interests. In the end we both found ourselves enthusiastic members of the University's Black Power Movement.

One afternoon it's-a-say-hulloto-your-neighbour-day student walked up to me in front of the library and congratulated me for topping the class in History of Science and Technology. I gave her no response. She withdrew, first searching for words that never escaped her mouth, then confoundedly forcing her guilty-conscious cheeks to form a smile which was instantly soaked up by her sudden perspiration. She shook her head gently and walked away, to join a group of talkative students not far from me. From there she stole two or three glances at me, but always using the group as a shield.

J.C.M. Joe, being in the group, walked up to me and flicked his fingers over my eyes. I did not blink. He flicked his fingers again. Still, there was no response from me.

"Hey, ei, ei, Ei," he shouted. "What's this? What's this? What's the meaning of this? Eh? Brother keeping a secret from a brother in broad daylight like this? Come, come now, man. Don't be a misinare. What did she say? What did she say?"

He ambled around me, with his hands at his back, eyeing me up and down, then walking faster and majestically like a cock about to lose its feathers. Letting his dimples curve deeper into his cheeks, he laughed: "Oho, ho, ho. So. So. So this is how the world goes round, eh? Secret whispers on a broad daylight like this then comes the night and the usual toils and sweat of the odd man out. The usual launching of Apollo Ten into the middle of the earth with that formidable weapon of the man himself. Aio Mamo Ghosti-ehe. Come on, man. Don't keep the sad world in suspense. I saw her whisper it to you."

For days, for weeks, for months now, Just Call Me Joe had been using the same jokes and everyday colloquialism to enlighten me. I had often wondered how I could go on breathing without his companionship.

"She's your size, brother - you know, same build, same height, length and depth, age perhaps, same everything else except she's got two brave, fat muscles on her chest for protection against you and - and -"

"Oh, go away," I said, irritated.

"Oh, I see, I see," said J.C.M. Joe, pretending to look hurt. "You're in one of those moods again, eh?" He laughed. "Make sure don't overdoeth it, son. It's no good for the mindeth. Laugh whenst thou art depresseth and crieth when thy heart's filleth with happinesseth. Aio, Sodom and Gomorraheth."

I turned away from him.

When I turned around a moment later he was possessively watching the girl who, by now, had been left alone by the other students. The students, with books tucked under their arms, walked away in different directions, laughing, jeering and exchanging friendly abuses.

J.C.M. Joe nudged me roughly and whispered: 'Hey you know what, tambu - I mean, brother - just call me Joe - she's not bad, not bad at all, ah? Not bad for a pot, I mean. I mean, you could just hold her thus and oh brother, oh brother, oohh...'

An elderly gentleman, in his late sixties by my judgment, white-haired, with slightly high-cheek bones which revealed the glory of crimson tropical sunbaths and wearing a snow-white, walrus moustache, walked up to the girl and started talking to her. The girl just giggled, looking every now and then in our direction, then at the concrete matting beneath her, then back at the gentleman's face again. Both J.C.M. Joe and I watched from afar as they talked, hearing only the loud and coy giggles from the girl. Their mouths opened and closed, like two puppets on strings without the sound track to bring life into them; at least that is what I thought I was seeing, from a distance. Then the girl, still giggling, made two or three nods which looked like bows of humble respect and, with a few books tucked tightly under one arm, started walking towards us. We watched her movements; the slow and timid yet rhythmic strides of her slender legs, the flat motionless abdomen under her white and black floral dress, and the black eyes which seemed to focus on my feet and then rise slowly until... I looked away. A few seconds later, by that time she had reached the spot where we were standing, I heard J.C.M. Joe cough lightly, probably to her. She responded with a mumble which sounded like 'hullo' and I turned just in time to watch her walk on, along the pavement and into the maze of gigantic concrete pillars, posts, walls, and down a brief set of stairs which led one's eyes into the heart of many semi-lighted academic prison cells. I thought I saw her smiling to herself when she walked past us.

"She's your size," I heard J.C.M. Joe repeat himself behind me. "What a pity she's not deep enough for me."

I moved away from him. "Hey, ei, ei, ei, Ei," he shouted. "What's the meaning of this, eh? Shit, don't tell me it's brother walking out on brother on a hot day like this. It's too hot, man; too hot. You can't just walk away sweating for nothing."

A little away from him I let my eyes fly all around me; to the empty space above, to a nearest brick wall, to my feet, to J.C.M. Joe who grinned, then to the gentleman. The gentleman stood alone, but was now walking as if he was in search of another soul for communication.

I walked back to Just Call Me Joe.

"What was it that you were telling me?" I asked.

"When?" he returned.

I was surprised to see that he was not bored by my indifference at all.

"About three months ago."

"Shit, man. Be specific, be specific. We are at Uni, remember."

"You said I had reasons enough to start hating some people," I returned, almost angrily.

"Remember? Back in the room, when I first came to the campus and when we were talking about the death of Enita."

"Who's Enita?"

"Mother."

"Oh that."

Just Call Me Joe laughed.

"Well, you see," he then said, "it's hard to say, really."

He put a finger over his lips and pretended to think. The gentleman who had been talking to the girl now began walking towards us, frightfully appearing too important for me. Just Call Me Joe waved to him and made as if to go forward and meet him. "No come on, brother," he said instead, "your must know." I thought he would grow impatient with me but he wasn't. "No, I mean, a fellow like you who thinks a lot, who gets A's and B's in most subjects, who tops the class in H.S.T., who gets secret whispers from little Uni. Girls should know. I mean, there are certain things you must hate, certain things that caused Enita's death for instance - if you know what I mean - certain things that kept you away from her since your childhood, certain things that make you feel you have no home, no friends, no people to look at and say I'm one of you... I mean, man... You can't go loving the world forever, gees."

"I don't hate, J.C.M. Joe," I said, sounding like a mouse crying out to the deaf wide world. "No, I don't hate; you must understand that. If there was hate in me, any hate at all, it would never be for any man in particular. It would be directed to the attitudes of people around me; to what they say without much thought of how much damage their so-called words of wisdom can cause to whoever they talk to, like, perhaps Father Jefferson whose love for the school and the country made me, and others besides, betray my own people - or simply like a student I came across today who was too busy yapping away like a lost puppy about how important he was, he couldn't listen to a poor prelim student's views ... So you see, J.C.M. Joe, I would only have that much to hate as a man; but I would never ever in all the seventeen years of my life have

the guts to hate another man. Well, I sound a bit of a misinare here
but what I'm trying to say is that I have no hate nor love for others;
I mean, I marvel at people, like Enita, but I can't compliment
them, which shouldn't be mistaken as hate, nor another way of
looking at..."

"Fillin ourait, mait?" a voice, rather coarse in its attempted
imitation of the Aussie accent, startled me from behind and I turned
abruptly to be confronted by three grinning black faces."Yu oukai,
mait?" was the inquiry again, and I realized it came from a student
standing closer to me. He grinned, perhaps awaiting a reply from
me. Tired of waiting he nudged the others and, half-covering his
mouth with the back of his open palm as children do lest they
be heard by the people they talk about, he laughed and said, "Ei
fellas, dis kid's gon saikos o samting; i was tokin tu'imself. Ihi,
hi, he, he, ha ha."

A lady, one of the lecturers' typists I had imagined, walked
past and gave me a smile which read 'Yeah, I know you. Ha-
ha,' and strolled on. Then I noticed that Just Call Me Joe had
abandoned me.

I found him talking with the elderly gentleman in front of the
chemistry lab. Upon seeing me J.C.M. Joe beckoned.

"Here he is," I heard him say to the gentleman as I approached
them. "Brother," said J.C.M. Joe with a bow then turned and bowed
again to the gentleman, "this is Mr. Goldsworth; Mr. Goldsworth,
our ex-Deputy Head Prefect of All Saints'."

"Yes of course, of course," said Mr. Goldsworth, extending
his hand. "I'm more than delighted, my lad..." I felt the firm,
humanitarian squeeze. "I have been looking forward to meeting
you, my boy. And I must say..."

I let my mouth wide agape, thinking of suitable words to say
and at the same time drowning the gentleman's words with my
sudden shock of bafflement. But no words came out of me. Why,
this is Archiebald Goldsworth, "in person", whose name appears
prominently in the history books of our old school; for whom we
prayed every year on All Saints' Day and sometimes saluted or
bowed before his portrait; and without whom most of us would

never have had the chance to acquire the education we now have. And there he was, right in front of me, smiling and letting those blue eyes survey my profile with friendliness and paternity. I just did not know what to say.

"Mr. Goldsworth," I managed to say at length, "I-I'm -I'm proud to be an old boy of All Saints'." Somehow, deep inside my heart, I felt that what I had just said was true. For the first time, it seemed, I felt the paradox of my whole life: of always wanting to go on walking in one direction, only to turn back remembering that there are also people like me; of always arguing, raising contradictory views, with an imaginary Father Jefferson in my dreams then walking out on him, slamming the door hard on his face and running wild into the webs of the wide free world, escaping one net of confusion just to be caught in another; just to return to him a few years later in a complete distorted state of mind and say, "Yes, Father, you were saying..."

"I am glad to hear you say that, my boy," Mr. Goldsworth said.

He paused, looked at each one of us closely, then transfixed his stare at something somewhere behind us. His face showed an expression worn by dedicated men of the world in deep contemplation.

"Yes, my lads," he then continued in a faraway voice, "yes; yes, yes, yes..."

Mr. Goldsworth turned his face away from Just Call Me Joe and me. He began now pacing the pavement with heavy trods, his hands behind his back with the fingers meeting and caressing each other into light locks. We followed him: with J.C.M. Joe wondering what was in my mind and I listening attentively for the next words.

"I have received a number of letters from the Principal of All Saints'," he said, still walking ahead of us and never looking back, "and each letter is an expression of deepest concern - not only from Father Jefferson but also from friends of the school here, in Australia, in England and in America too - of the vitality of education in this country. So much need there is for education for those who come after you, so much work there is to be done and so much money to be raised for the erection of the school's permanent buildings."

We followed the gentleman meekly, listening attentively.

"I am sure what I am saying is nothing new to you, my lads," the old man's voice came again, "since you two have been to All Saints' - and I am sure you do recognize the needs of the school."

"Yes... yes, Mr. Goldsworth," J.C.M. Joe agreed.

"A man, my lads," Mr. Goldsworth continued, "a man alone cannot go about slicing a piece of cake on his own. There must be other men, dedicated men of the same interests, men with enthusiasm and responsibility, men who are homogeneous in their common conscience, causes and so forth, to help take up the yoke the lone man has and help slice the cake to plenty for the benefit and betterment of all."

Nostalgia gripped my insides and in the distant parts of my mind I could hear a familiar voice calling "*Qui bono?*" and I responding at the top of my voice "*Ergo!*"

"To put it another way," the old man continued walking towards the library, "there must be co-operation from those who hold the upper hand and those who hold the lower; to have them work together in achieving this country's nationhood and unity and this can only be done through education, my lads, education."

"Educate them all," J.C.M. Joe said. He said this so suddenly and unexpectedly that I was both startled and afraid of Mr. Goldsworth.

The elderly gentleman stopped when we had reached the steps that fell to the student forum or arena where the student politicians aired their views, still having his back on us. Ahead of us emerged a few students who were now busily moving from door to door, going in for, and coming out from, lectures and tutorials.

"A popular example of what I am trying to stress now," said the old man, turning right and away from the steps to the forum, "and it's quite often used at All Saints', is this: a twig alone can be easily broken; but where there are more than twenty twigs gathered and bundled together it will be hard to break them'.

Consider then, my lads, that each twig is a person working for a particular purpose. Now then, and this is very tricky, would one twig last?" He paused, to allow us time to grasp the meaning of the parable. "That, my lads, that is what I want you to think about; for through this ideology, simple though it may seem, a society or a country stands fast on its own. And remember, lads, remember that without this form of co-operation a country, however big or small, will eventually bring itself to chaos, and there may not be room for those who will want to cry over its spilt milk."

The statement of the century, I thought sadly.

Mr. Goldsworth turned to confront us.

"I am growing old, my lads," he announced in a crisp voice; "yes; I am growing old. And some day, one day, I shall cease to be." He paused again, to let the sentiment sink into our hearts. "Yes, yes, rather an uncomfortable experience that all humanity must go through. But what matter... At times, I am inclined to think that within a man there is a certain duty, a certain promise, that must be fulfilled for a certain purpose before the end."

"Yes, Mr. Goldsworth, we realize that," said J.C.M. Joe.

"I have gone through all walks of life in my time," the old man turned away again, jutting his snowy head ever heavenwards, "and this, to an extent, enables me to assert bravely that know how things are, will be, must be. My experiences in the last war, for instance, had dawned on me the realization of all wonders a man can see in this world, certain sacrifices he must make for a particular cause or causes."

Just Call Me Joe nudged me to show me a broad grin between his dimpled cheeks. I followed closely the footsteps of Mr. Goldsworth to the library, as he spoke with authority and care.

"Twenty-five years ago I would have died," he said; "yes, my lads, I would have died if only God had not put me in the hands of those villagers without whose help I would have ended up ignorant of the meaning of my life. It was then that I saw things, and thought of doing something to help the poor villagers."

And I thought back, turning the pages of the old school's history, and through Mr. Goldsworth's speech I could lucidly see the villagers bearing a fatally wounded warrior on a stretcher to safety, half-humming, half-cooing *Onward Christian Soldiers.*

"There was something they needed but they knew nothing about," Mr. Goldsworth went on; "they had to see the light while they had the chance. And somehow I felt it was my duty to see to it that they possessed this light as rightly and as much as any other human being upon this earth."

"Of course, of course," put in J.C.M. Joe, as if talking to the students ahead of us.

Whether Mr. Goldsworth heard him, I could not tell, for he kept walking towards the library.

"When I started talking about starting a school it was a one-man job at first due of course to financial shortages and lack of interest from the people who should recognize what I had recognized. Then I had offers, mainly from Churches in Australia, England and America, which sent teachers in my stead, men and women, dedicated men and women, who were prepared to carry out my principles and, if possible, put them to fruitful practice. But alas, alas, some of these men and women died as martyrs and saints while trying to bring the light to the villagers some of whom might have participated twenty-five years ago in saving me. Yet, these men and women who died, had to die; they had to die, my lads, in order to have the villagers themselves open their eyes to see the light."

For no reason at all I suddenly caught myself thinking of Jimi Damebo. A random memory, random memory, I immediately dismissed the thought.

"And every time I think of the school itself," went on Mr. Goldsworth, "there is something to add to it, my lads, something more... So you see, All Saints' is, in many ways, part of me, part of a man's life, one might say; it isn't a gesture of mere gratitude to what the villagers had done for me during the last war. No. All Saints' is, in so many ways, my child."

By this time we had reached the door of the library. A group of students walked past us: some held up clenched fists in the air and called out 'Black Power' to Just Call Me Joe who grinned; others just giggled and hurried on after the comments '*Ei taim bipo, i pinis nau, lapun,*' to Mr. Goldsworth who showed no response; and still others exchanged conspicuous secret glances and remarked, 'Ai luk, dat's da kid u was tokin tu'imself. Yeah, dat's im ourait. A saiko kais.' Mr. Goldsworth turned slowly, still deep in thought if he didn't hear the comments, to face us both. He rubbed his bushy, white eyebrows free of perspiration and blinked two or three times as if he had at last discovered what was written in our hearts. J.C.M. Joe waved to some students. I looked up at the old man.

"But I must say I was more than glad to hear you say you are proud of the school, my lad," he directed the words more to me than to J.C.M. Joe. "Bear in mind, young sir," he added, "that if ever a country needs development and prosperity it is young people like you who must be its leaders, who must be its means of attaining its economic, social, political and perhaps cultural and religious integrity. It is through you that it will become a nation, a strong united nation."

I listened in silence, thankful to learn that I would be one of the leaders of the country. Suddenly the old man shook his head vigorously as if awakening from reverie.

"Well, I have talked too much," he said, and playfully threw a powerful fist, which tickled my belly. "We'll have to talk about the school some other time, my friends." He smiled down at me. "How nice to see you. I must declare you are a cunning little chap because every time I come here you don't seem to be around, and I have been hunting for you all through last week, asking Joseph where you were and all he could say was "Oh well, he's around but you only find him asleep in his bed late at nights." He turned to J.C.M. Joe, laughing. "And how's our Black Power man? Always addressing himself as 'Just Call Me Joe'. Yes, good old happy days. Reminds me of my own academic years when the students at the university I went to, could divide themselves into different groups of Rightism, Leftism, this and that, aha, ha, ha. Yes, yes, there never were times much happier than one's academic years."

Mr. Goldsworth danced as he spoke, like a boxer in a ring, throwing his playful punches at me then at J.C.M. Joe.

"Well, if you two don't have anything to do tonight," he danced to me then to J.C.M. Joe, "would you care to come to dinner at my place?"

"Be delighted, Mr. Goldsworth," I dodged his playful punches and looked up to J.C.M. Joe who nodded and put on his usual grin again. "Oh, that's right," I said, sparring dutifully with the old man, "today's Friday. Yes, we'd like to come but please don't feel obliged to take us in, Mr. Goldsworth."

"There is absolutely nothing to it, my lads. Nothing at all."

"Any beer?" asked Just Call Me Joe who was too slow to dodge the old man's heavy arm which landed paternally on his shoulders.

"Oho, Joseph. Always talking about beer. I can imagine seeing you in a few years time, young man. An influential politician and a giant of a man, all because of beer."

The dinner was profoundly delicious. Classy would perhaps be the right word. There were paw-paw drinks, fruit salad, sugared banana and custard, some taro and *kaukau* and a variety of imported vegetables enriched with coconut oil, sauces and gravy of both Oriental and Western tastes. Meat was in abundance and there was enough grog to last anyone with any amount of drinking appetite the whole night. It was more a party than dinner, as most dinners are to some influential people in Moresby.

A lot of people came to the Goldsworth dinner that night. There were university students and members of the academic and administrative staff: members of the House, ordinary people; senior public servants, junior clerks; guests of distinction, and of *lusman bilong* rot. They swarmed in merrily in Afro-Asian shirts, in baggy long pantaloons: round-necked T-shirts, white spotless shirts: cheap looking thongs, high-heeled shoes: dusty old Hush Puppies, black shiny boots. It was a night for all to socialize: some people talked of the past with regret, others talked of the bright future; some talked politics, others talked culture; some cried for some unknown reasons after a few bottles of beer, others just laughed with everybody else; a few danced casually, or did the *tapiokwa* dance as the Trobriand islanders call it, to the rhythm of the music that came out from one of the rooms, and yet others got drunk" to kill human sensitivity. Mr. Goldsworth was the happiest man that night. A satisfied man, with the usual bright and young personality, moving lightly from guest to guest like a butterfly, cracking a joke here, participating in a vital political discussion there; offering a beer here, amicably slapping a *haus boi* there. A senior public service acquaintance of his had once described him as 'a worthy man, a great man of our country' the compliment we remembered so well from the mouth of our History Master at All Saints'. And there never was a guest who later left the gathering without a word or two with the old man.

After watching Mr. Goldsworth for some time I could not resist wishing I were as content as he, in a way I had been wishing all my life, never stopping once to admit that my life was full of silent dreams of a world only I could feel, think about and live in. This particular world was so alien, so incurable if it were a disease that my hopes for the future had turned out to be those of fear, uncertainty, confusion, and self-destruction. And the terror of it all was my own refusal to find ways of surpassing such a curse. It became part of me, my habit, my badge of honor, but a concept for which no other strong enough belief could help erase my internal stubbornness. I still was the *lusman* at heart.

Mrs. Goldsworth was equally the happiest woman that night, entertaining the guests with the same amount of enthusiasm as the old man. She offered drinks to guests of all sorts, escorted some, the latecomers, to the dining room to devour the unending surplus of food, as well as shared and cracked jokes, conversed and cackled with them. Every now and then she would answer her old friends' questions on how young Jack Goldsworth was doing at the A.N.U., inform them that he was expected 'home next Christmas after completing his Masters', or briefly and unobligingly outline to the interested newcomers, like J.C.M. Joe and myself, her husband's history from the days of his youth to that night in Port Moresby.

I discovered, after moving among the crowd, that I had unconsciously consumed four bottles of beer. Fears of complete insecurity and self-betrayal began stalking my conscience. I knew that a rather rapid consumption of beer for a starter like me was not at all rewarding. Yet I felt at the same time that I needed some kind of release, an inner release. As such I moved about at ease amid the din of the gathering, with some difficulty at first but tactically afterwards, no longer afraid of the dangers of self-exposure, thinking I had no choice but to pretend to live with the crowd; by the time I was tipsy I felt secure.

Just Call Me Joe, to my surprise, had come out of the Goldsworth castle talking louder than usual. Surprisingly still, he came out holding hands with a dim dim who was wearing a pair of liquor-crimson eyes that flickered freely at any mobile male in the gathering as if some magic had gotten into the dear daughter of the soil. At last, at last, I thought drunkenly, we have a *lusmeri* in our midst.

"You arc not enjoying yourself," I heard someone speak behind me. I looked around to find the old man towering over me. I understood then that he was superior.

"Oh yes I am, Mr Goldsworth," I returned. "But please don't bother about me."

"And er, don't take too much of that brown and green stuff," the old man joked in an imitated Aussie accent, then strolled off. I admired him, 'Man is a social animal'?

A lady, the same typist I saw in front of the library, walked up to me and wc talked. After some time she recommended that I should read Colin Johnson's *Wild Cat Falling*.

"Why?" I asked. "Because it was written by a half-caste?"

She left.

Then Just Call Me Joe walked over to me with his friend.

"Her name is La," he shouted and slapped me hard on the back. I felt my back hurt from the 'pum' of his palm.

"Who's La?" asked the dim dim.

"La?" enquired Just Call Me Joe, which proved that he too was drunk.

"Who is La?" again the Australian asked, slowly, as if a flood of jealousy was surging through her blood.

"Oh La," shouted J.C.M. Joe in sudden realisation. "Of course, of course. Er, La is his fiance -"

"Bullshit," I said.

"Oh by the way," said J.C.M. Joe; "brother, this is Sophie."

Then he gave the *dim dim* my Christian name after which she said, "Oh that's you, ah brother? Ah, my *wantok, yu yet -yu winim olgeta*."

We shook hands. I felt I liked Sophie.

"Who was this La that you were talking about?' she asked a while later.

"Oh, it's the name of a girl at Uni., Sophie," explained J.C.M. Joe. "Also prelim, like me and him here."

"I see. What about her?"

"She's interested in this *doga*."

"Well, wish you tons of luck, comrade," smiled Sophie and tapped me on the shoulder.

"I wish I could thank you for that, my wantok, but J.C.M. Joe is a cold-blooded liar."

"*Aio Goudi*," laughed J.C.M. Joe mockingly. He then said, "Hey, Sophie, I'm going to piss."

"Okay, but don't fall asleep in the John."

"In the what?" asked J.C.M. Joe.

"In the John."

"What the hell's that?"

"That's someone's *tok ples* for the dyke pot."

"Oh," said J.C.M. Joe and let out an uproarious laugh that drew attention from the other guests.

I was afraid I would become sober again.

"Go on," said Sophie, ignoring the stares around us. "Go on, before you wet your pants, Just Call Me Joe."

Just Call Me Joe staggered into the enclosures of the Goldsworth haven to release the poison he had just consumed.

Sophie turned and stared at me, her pupils enlarged, revealing slight crimson tinges that glittered under the soft neon lights.

That happens, I thought sadly; at beer parties. She leaned forward to let her cigarette fumes cloud my line of vision.

"Just Call Me Joe tells me you write some of the stuff for his forums," she said.

"Well, some of the ideas are mine, but a lot of them are J.C.M. Joe's own thinking. I don't contribute much, really." I stopped, to have a silent opinion on her but dismissed the thought. "They are a village idiot's confused, studentship convivialities, really," I then said.

"Oh, but some of the stuff J.C.M. Joe says are real -I mean, they project the facts of the whites - well, take his forum yesterday, for instance; what was it called again?"

"Looking Into Ourselves."

"Ah, that's it," said Sophie.

She offered me a cigarette. I told her I wasn't a smoker yet. "I really enjoyed listening to it," she continued. "Somehow I felt that speech was far removed from the Movement's other speeches in that it created that sense of depth and clear understanding of what it means to be black, a subservient of some huge churning machine that sort of hypnotises you or something. It was a creative piece of speech, anyway." Pause. No sign of Just Call Me Joe. What's Sophie explaining. "Tell me, do you really believe in Black Power?"

"What do you want me to say to that, Sophie?"

"Well, it's a straight forward question, isn't it?"

"I know."

I felt my head spin.

"I mean, do you really think, judging from yesterday's forum, that the black Niuginian is somewhat undergoing the torments that are very much different from those that the African and American Negro goes through?"

"Different? I reckon all blacks are black—they can even be white and vice versa - but the torments, which must be spiritual if not psychological, are always there, within anyone, as a basis of all human suffering; very near to sadism, but not—definitely not—within sadism, since this its a developing country—this is Papua New Guinea—much as what J.C.M. Joe spoke of yesterday."

"Yes—but don't you think that is sadism still no matter how much you might strive to avoid, let's say, sexual and other perverse obsessions that should still reflect sadism, or are forms of sadism, anyway. I mean, let's face it: I can just take one look at you and know what's in that little head of yours. It is sadism."

"But you must realize the importance of having to leave, in your definition, an individual Niuginian at the very doorstep of sadism."

"You underestimate your own people."

"There is none that convinces me I am no better," I said. And in sudden anger, I added, "You mustn't force them forward too quickly, please. Don't give them easy promotions..."

"Strewth," laughed Sophie, throwing her bead back. I looked all around me uneasily. "You arc not being kind to" she paused, surveyed my profile then completed the phrase—your people."

"You don't have to listen to me, Sophie," I said, thinking, I'm not educated enough; I'm still immature; I'm still Enita's useless, seventeen year-old silence and perversity. O James, Jimi Damebo, where are you? I envy your intelligence, your serenity that knows no guilt. "But a restless Niuginian, now, isn't someone who indulges in the pleasures of pain from internal suffering. None would, anyway, let alone have him or her just imitate the beauty and satisfaction seen in the Christian tradition of martyrdom. Rather, even in his prime of—what?—having achieved or reached tertiary education and having acquired raison d'etre to glorify his personality, in reality, he still is that young Christian moralist."

"An atheist and a Christian at once."

"Almost, Sophie: a profound Christian rejecting Christianity, rejecting himself. And a closer look at his self can easily reveal that he is a pretentious village nut. So in his self-rejection he is rejecting the self that is not his. And the result after the absence of this particular self, which is Christianity, is his original self which is void, but an emptiness that is filled by fruitless nostalgia for an unknown traditional past. Sometimes, though, such an emptiness could enable him to start patching up his own being. Not many Papua New Guineans, not even your Just Call Me Joe, recognize that."

"Hell, you must be some kind of a philosopher or something," said Sophie.

I saw her eyes roll lazily, her head sway a little and her shoulders sag after a deep sigh.

"I can't think any more," she lied.

I liked Sophie.

The cold neon lights from the Goldsworth Garden of Eden began to spin before me. I forgot concentration. Yet an instinct warned me to keep on going until I had not only reached but also crossed a thick dividing line between sanity and insanity. I knew I would still be alive then. And what would be there to confront me, had I crossed the line even in my state of sub-conscious yet distinct, even faint, living mind?

Peace? Tranquility? Getting drunk was a stimulating exercise for the mind.

I rose. I needed another beer.

"Sorry?" mumbled Sophie.

"I need another beer."

"Oh. Get two, please."

Just Call Me Joe met me on the way with three bottles. We sat down again just as the gathering was beginning to come to an end, due to the din which was louder than was perhaps expected. People began leaving one by one and I realized it was time for us to go.

"Is Mr. Goldsworth arranging transport for us, J.C.M. Joe?" I asked, uncomfortably beginning to feel sober.

"Oh, he will drive us," offered Sophie, and leaned over just Call Me Joe to pick out a straw that was caught in his tightly-knotted hair. She missed the straw and found herself laughing against his tough body.

"Hey, come on, let's piss off," said J.C.M. Joe, after watching the crowd for awhile.

"Just Call Me Joe?"

"Yes, Sophie?"

"Our friend's pretty simple, isn't he? I mean, he doesn't find it hard in bringing himself out to the open, or something. Hey, wantok," Sophie then turned to me, "If I were in your clothes I'd feel like strolling down the streets with my fingers chokingly gripping my own neck. Release yourself, man; release yourself."

"Yeah," said J.C.M. Joe, almost defending me; "he's the only knowledgeable idiot we have around here." But he was watching a Bougainvillian student who had somehow come to bad terms with a *dim dim*.

"Hey, watch where you are gaing, whitey," shouted the Buka student while picking himself off the ground.

"Well, if you weren't too bloody drunk, you'd watch where you were going, mate," retorted the Aussie.

"Don't speak to me like that, whitey," shouted back the Buka student and reached for the other's collar; the Australian's spectacles fell to the ground during his unsuccessful attempt to jump clear. "Come on, someone - hold my beer while I fix this white bastard a lesson." His friends joined him but were struggling to pull him away.

"Come on, Camillo," they chorused. "Leave the guts-ache alone. He's too fat to fight for himself."

"Leave me be, idiots," shouted Camillo. "I want to know why he called me black bastard before he tripped me. Oh yes, brothers, I want to know. I need to know. Come on, whitey - explain yourself, or I swear by my ancestors I'll spill your blood here and now."

"Come on, Camillo," moaned his friends; "let's piss off."
"What for?" cried J.C.M. Joe suddenly, startling Sophie and me.
"Are you kids women to let the bastard get away with it? I heard
him call Camillo Mungkas bastard."

"He what?" the Bougainvillians responded in startled anger,
thus releasing Camillo.

"He called him Mungkas bastard," shouted J.C.M. Joe. He
was grinning. "Now let me call all of you lot Mungkas bastards
and see if it doesn't hurt. Go on, Mungkas bastard. Doesn't that
hurt? Ei, Ei? Go on, misinares—pissoofff."

At this opportunity Camillo rushed his victim. "And you know
what Mungkas means?" he shouted into the throat of the Aussie
gentleman. "Mungkas means black and black means power."

With the word "power" the student pushed the victim to the
ground and was about to ride him when there was a commotion
of hurrying figures, some of whom grabbed him in time. Someone
had managed to turn the music full blast; with the music the blacks
were off for their lives. They did not care who stood in their way:
they wanted to spill blood; they wanted to kill; they wanted to
survive, to live. Just Call Me Joe was within that black crowd.
Soon the rest of the gathering swarmed the trouble spot and Sophie
and I found ourselves within the group, holding hands. Alone
in the middle of the ring of the Mungkas the Aussie gentleman
became his own misfortune, his own poor condition, his own sad
destiny: he looked up to Sophie and me as if begging for mercy, as
if wanting us to go in and rescue him from the blacks. Speechless,
he stared at us expectantly. Calmly releasing my grip on Sophie, I
turned away.

"You are the one who rightly deserves the title of White
Fatherism," I heard Just Call Me Joe shout behind me. I turned,
like a traitor, to observe from a safe distance. "Yeah, we always
see you in the company of black people whom you are trying your
hardest to turn into another group of whites. You know what's
wrong with you? You are insecure, too damn alone to be free and
comfortable, a waif to be precise, who wants to be polite just for
the marvelment of blacks by whom you want to be thought of as

a good man, a simple good man, or some such shitthead rubbish as that. You are a wayward mariner who'd been washed ashore here and who has no soul, no beginnings, no nothing—you are empty inside, you hear? You are an exploiter, that's why you are too disagreeably fat. You are a moral teaching maniac, that's why you retreat every time a black man wants to approach you with something saner. The only blacks you want to be with are those that you think of as mere fools who must regard you as some *Bik Masta* beyond their comprehension. Understand? Understand me, white man. Go on, *raus*. Get out of my sight before I feel angry enough like my long gone ancestors to spill blood. Go on, away with you—you who turns my life into a dog-shitted venom." And Just Call Me Joe's words echoed eerily down the brightly lit yet silent Goldsworth Garden of Eden.

The music died.

Somehow J.C.M. Joe had managed to get the crowd under control. Sophie became hypnotized by Just Call Me Joe whose drunken and angry form in the middle of the crowd resembled the axis of a vast, yet dead, ferris wheel. In that instant I saw Mr. Goldsworth extend two powerful arms far in front of him, his face twisted into contours of pain supported by a popping pair of blazing eyes, yet remained where he was as if warned by some external command to keep still with the dead wheel.

The crowd became a snapshot, creating an atmosphere of a live, near-Rembrandtal abyss, although as soon as J.C.M. Joe resumed speaking, it slowly moved in, in lazy rhythm, all ears attentive.

"Away, away with you," continued J.C.M. Joe, lowering his voice to poetic tones. "For we know your kind, man. Come on, pick up your glasses and cause no more disgrace. You are simply a fool, a weakling at that." J.C.M. Joe paused to spit, and then raised his voice to a new and heightened kind of anger. "Ah, you know what you deserve as a name. But enough, enough of you, white man. The very sight of you turns the bile in my belly, so go on, on your way. Don't look back. Don't even dream of looking back. Away, away with you, into the privacy of your darkest dun-

geons among playboy magazines. Or pick up a random village
idiot along the road and produce useless bastards and *ol lusmmi
bilong rot.* That'll console you. That's all you shall deserve. And
don't use our society as an excuse to, hi'de from yours," J.C.M.
Joe laughed bitterly. "In fact, I've heard of people like you—I've
been to one of them's flat at Paga Hill. Man, he was so pissed he'd
pulled his uncle out in front of us and told us to help him flood
the floor with his manna of disgust from the heavens, ha. Yeah.
And his only reason had been that not even a local money-minded
bitch could love him. What an excuse. What a sumptuous state of
hog shit one can become, like a bloated bullfrog on a bad Sunday
and devoid of flesh, devoid of beauty."

Just Call Me Joe stopped to eye everyone at the gathering,
including Mr. and Mrs. Goldsworth. The tone of his voice had
again become calmer, more like a profound and concerned black
poet.

"Now all of you, listen to me," he said with deliberate care.
"You may think I'm mad. And yes, I can agree with you there—that
what I say is all madness. But the fear in it all is that everyone of
you might take my mania to be truth, the profound consequences
of which will be that of salvation for a nation from the self-cheated
noose of non-idealism, from the Australian Government itself
sending dogs like this fat slob here, from even our own so-called
politicians who commit themselves to this self-cheated noose of
non-idealism out of a false democracy that is completely white.
And the black man? What of him? Answer me, somebody."

He paused, his body quivering with the poetry of Negritude.

"Why, the black man that is of the soil is stripped, his youth far
molested, cursed and gripped by a slow, smoldering fire of colonial
hell, turning him into a mere grain of a sad case composed entirely
of senses that are too numb to respond; and the music of that
youth, that black youth, which is the soul of the forgotten village
is brought to a standstill. Why? Because of the perennial greed of
the white man that helps to do nothing but chop him down like a
tree, like that antique tree of time, like that."

Sophie drove us to the campus.

II

SPLIT-YOLK NOSTALGIA

It was another of those lethargic Friday afternoons for me. I wanted to stand in front of the library and become solidified. In that warmth, almost too humid of an atmosphere, I felt my insides uplifted by a certain desire that was not far removed from the wish Lot's wife had had when she wanted to take a last look at Sodom and Gomorrah (or Moresby?) and become petrified. A terrible wish, I thought, but I felt I wanted to do exactly that. Then my indifferent eyes caught a poster on the door of the library. It read: 'Dance. Dance. Dance. To the rhythm of Wanikaini. Tonite. Tonite. Tonite.' I let out the sigh of defeat.

"How about it?" J.C.M. Joe stalked from behind to startle me, indicating the poster.

"I am not coming, Just Call Me Joe."

"Oh come off it—I mean, pull yourself out of it, mate. Have some laughter in you for a change, will you? Gees kid, aren't you boring?" I tried to move away but he quickly jumped in my path.

"Gees, brother; you're too bloody – oh hell, I don't know. That girl's been eyeing you all week and the most you do is turn your back on her. Jesus Christ, son. Aren't you boring."

"I'm broke," I said, anxious to be left alone.

"And that's no excuse either because I'm paying for everybody tonight. You, me, Sophie and Sheila."

He left.

A number of students walked by, stolid, frozen-faced, like concrete pillars being moved around at random. Walking just after them to the side of the library I felt I was one of them, only if no one talked to me. So I kept myself at a safe distance.

When I rounded the corner that led to the bookshop I saw Sheila coming towards me. I stopped, froze. Beneath me I felt my feet move to the right, to the left, but there was no way of escape. If I turned suddenly and walked back pretending I had forgotten something in the library, the girl would sense the lie. I was trapped.

I leaned, instead, over the iron rail that joined the library and the bookshop, and bent my head further over the rail, suddenly wishing I were more than anonymous, non-existent. I felt the veins on my neck expand, causing me to sweat a little. Then I felt my eyes turn and sink deeper into the sockets until the polluted drain directly beneath became fogged before my vision. I was indeed forgetting the world, and in the distance I heard a faint scream of horror from a girl. The screams were let out repeatedly, somewhat clanging eerily, inaudibly at first but soon becoming like "Please, you. Do not die on me... you must not... it is important that you must not... no, you must not... you just cannot..."

Rather, it was Sheila Jivi La trying to say hello behind me for the fifth time, thus allowing me to conceal my own fantasy and, admittedly, sensuous internal complexities, by the reality of her physical presence.

"Hullo," she greeted me, for the sixth time.

"Good day."

"I said, hullo."

"Oh."

"Joseph tells me you lost Enita – was she your mother? Anyway, I am sorry."

"You needn't be." I did not bother to turn to her when I said this.

The sky at the back of the Arts/Law building was gradually turning into dark grey and I felt my spirits elevated, which was quite unnatural for me since dusk, something I had grown accustomed to, was at the back of me where Sheila was. And yes, it was growing dark; I turned, and straightened myself, confidently facing dusk again behind Sheila. It was as if it was her duty to wait for me to speak, although she was reading something from the last light of the fast-evanescing dusk.

I wondered if Sheila and I would be friends; lovers; spouses in marriage one day. Yet all thoughts of friendship with Sheila, to me, meant a university degree, a comfortable job with enough to eat, beautiful kids waking up fresh each 6.30 a.m. to jump on a sound sleeping 'Dadi', reminding him to wash before breakfast then rush off to the office before 7.45 a.m. after a brief kiss with 'Mama' Sheila, come home at 4.30 p.m. for another brief kiss with 'Mama' Sheila and the kids before washing the car for the weekend's trip to a picnic at Sogeri, *aoh Dirava.* All these constituted that inevitable feeling of hesitance in me. In order to need Sheila I had to choose between the world of pretences and deep essentialities of my being; one had to gain the qualifications to be something and something else. I wanted to be human.

True, the youthful body of Sheila was appealing; I could never deny that. I was even tempted to move forward and touch her and have it all done with. I did, thinking, 'It is now or never'.

"What are you reading, Mary?" I found myself asking her instead.

"Oh, some writing," replied Sheila. "I am not artistically minded but I like reading things that make you feel something rather than want to appreciate them like Shakespeare. I like this." She held out the foolscap towards me. "It is written by one of the the third year students. Do you want to have a look at it?"

I took the piece of paper and read the writing through. At first the whole poem was meaningless to me until I came across a familiar name.

"Why, Sophie wrote this," I exclaimed.

"Do you know her?"

"Oh yes. She drove us to the campus from Goldsworth's last Friday night. I think she and J.C.M. Joe are friends."

"Yes. Sophie told me about the dinner. Did you almost have a fight?"

"I can't fight, Sheila."

She laughed. "But Sophie told me Mr Goldsworth was upset with some of you."

"Oh yes, yes. He's the founder of All Saints'. By the way, did J.C.M. Joe tell you about All Saints'?"

"He did not have to. Your school is the outstanding school in Papua New Guinea. I should be proud if I went to a school like yours. What a pity it is not co-ed."

"Most people say so."

"And it is true. It must be gratifying for you to hear so many people talking about the school. I even heard a Literature tutor say that most All Saints' graduates, all of them in fact, are very much 'Englishmanlike'. I mean, in your speech, your manners, general social etiquette... "

"That's because most of the teachers are English. Even the Principal is English, and it's not always so easy not having to sing those old songs with touches of nostalgia in them like the 'Bonnie Banks' or those 'Green Isles' for which one's 'thoughts are ever yearning'. You know, when I was in Form one I used to think of my home as having 'green isles' and 'bonnie banks' with rich pastures where sheep roamed, with my imaginary father as the shepherd or something..."

"It is hard, brother," said Sheila slowly. "It is hard." I wondered what she meant by that. Then holding me by the shoulders with a certain kind of urge, she said, "But I cannot understand why you are so quiet, so far away and well, unlike Joseph, you keep yourself to yourself."

"I was born to be that way, Sheila," I said, feeling uncomfortable about talking of myself. "It's—it's my life, it's part of me—I was born of it." Remembering James St Nativeson, I sighed and added, "But anyway, people like us die like frogs on the road..." I was on the verge of growing impatient again.

"Then you would disagree with those who regard silence as terrifying?"

Now who was it, I reflected; was it Louis Stevenson who claimed that?

"No, I wouldn't disagree, Sheila," I then said. "It's inevitable — it's – it's not my fault that I must have deep respect for silence."

She withdrew her hands from my shoulders.

"Did you like Sophie's poem?" she asked a little later.

"Oh yes."

"She says she will send it to someone she knows in Melbourne who will turn it into a popular song."

"That's good. But I'm surprised it has to be Sophie writing a poem like this."

"What do you mean?"

"I don't know – in many ways it makes me feel guilty. I just don't know, Sheila."

"Why, brother? Because you are in the Black Power activities with Joseph?"

"No. I just feel Sophie's too innocent to write something like this. She's feeling somebody else's guilt."

Why has fate
borne me white? My meanings are void.
I have none to fear but my own fear of fearing.
The pains you endure I breathe in to create
a new birth as in a new child; the cry you weep
only brings out my shame; the truth I feel melts
still to a pool of guilt that is not mine - yet how,
how can I discharge my internal river of human
significance
my only hope
to flow down your carpet of red,
along your road to freedom?
A mother's wishes rejected, a father's glory
washed down the drain of justice, and I remain
stripped free, alone, but wishing...

"Sophie is having problems with her boyfriend," explained Sheila, as I re-read the poem under the lights that came from the library to announce it was dark already. "She just broke up with her *Bougain villian* boyfriend and she feels upset about it. It is sad. I think it also has something to do with Joseph, if the two of them are serious." Sheila paused, only to add sadly, "I would like to help these people. Somehow."

Why do people write poems? Why does Jimi Damebo write poetry? Why does Sophie?

> *Man*
> *Can I hide myself in you?*
> *I have come here to turn my back*
> *On the world outside which cries out*
> *My shame and guilt -*
> *Be my blind leading the blind,*
> *Unseeing the road you take,*
> *Still, let me walk beside you*
> *Lead me on, lead me on...*

"These Australians must be feeling the same things we would feel if we were living in their society," said Sheila.

"What do you mean—if we were living in their society? We already are living in their society." I was again beginning to feel both impatient and agitated. "It's this stupid rat race business. Absolute shithouse of an unnecessary suffering," I thought quietly.

> Absurdity being my guide
> I shall journey on and on
> into the dark abyss
> of sweet nothingness
> as was...

"Well, did you talk to her?

"Yes, J.C.M. Joe."

"What do you think of her?"

"She speaks careful English."

"And what did she say in her careful English?"

"She gave me Sophie's poem to read."

"So you haven't asked her to the dance—right?"

"Right."

"Christ, kid. Now I feel obligated to go and ask her myself for you. Christ the King of all kings, son. Aren't you boring."

I was surprised to see a certain amount of change in Just Call
Me Joe. Somehow, his "christs" and "kids" and "sons" began to
baffle me. He turned to the door of our room.

"Just Call Me Joe."

"Yes?"

"Did you read what Sophie wrote?"

Closing the door after him, and from outside, J.C.M. Joe spoke
with deliberate care, "Don't misunderstand me, brother." I was
trying to make out a dark form of him through the partly opened
louvers. "Tell me, brother, have you ever imagined yourself caught
in a storm, your canoe shattered to smithereens, and you had
only the outrigger to boat you and your family, then discovered
suddenly that there was also someone else near you struggling to
live?" At the words "someone else" I thought of the Captain of
Quartz and the sea of solitude, of a woman called Enita, of Mary,
of Yaguyawa-Kuburina so vacant and meaningless to me, of the
Mungkas Bougainvillian who called out to the white society in
anger that he too should live, and—Sophie? What about that
village elder living in the dry parts of the Goldsworth District?
There was a long moment of silence from J.C.M. Joe in which I
imagined myself alone in the sea of solitude, away from the rest
of the world, but not caught in a storm. I wondered if J.C.M. Joe
had left, but then his voice came in again through the louvres,
"An outrigger after the storm is not enough. There has got to be a
different and a bigger world—a new world. There has got to be."
Which wasn't just a plea from Just Call Me Joe; it was his big
promise of our future.

Heart-thudding, deep-toned drum beats and local
improvisations of modern popular songs from the 'Wanikaini'
exploded in me and turned themselves into colourful girandoles
of tremor-riddled, frenzy-flurry replacements of the many, many
things that were missing in my life. Sheila and Sophie danced on
one side while J.C.M. Joe and I responded from the other. Soon the
Students' Union Hall was crowded by a new breed of youths, all

doing the Negro-ghetto go-gos with their own improvisations or twirls of the human body based on traditional village movements.

The lights changed, the electric guitars whined and meowed wild, and a new wave of spirit swept along the several lines of bobbing paired-dancers. Everyone shrieked, cheered, did a variety of movements that could stimulate a bystander to the point of tumescence, and generally fluttered and winged like fowls trying to fly to the air of freedom, as the lights darkened further, turning the hall into an atmosphere of a dark, reddish glowing cave which gave me the internal comfort to breathe at ease.

"I thought you could not dance," Sheila Jivi La shouted. "And look at you. You are smiling."

At intervals, however, I had very brief, single-worded conversations with her, all of them having to do with my topping the class in History of Science and Technology which made it hard for me to see the sense in Sheila and I being together as a happy pair for the University's Friday night social gatherings. I was only afraid I would turn around in the end of that social evening and tell her that I didn't ask her to come to me. But at least for the moment I was free of Father Jefferson, Mr Goldsworth and some prowlers who were always eager to recommend for me the sentiments of 'wild cats falling'.

During one round of a random slow waltz, Sheila leaned forward as if to kiss me, but spoke into my ear that Darwin was a fool because he had 'contradicted the Church and that no one in the world would be willing to be classed as a second-hand monkey'. I thought I heard that remark about Darwin somewhere before. But she said she was proud to hear I had obtained an 'A' grading for an essay on Darwin's theory. She explained she did not know why she felt proud of me and I thought, 'Bullshit.'

"Darwin was only speaking on probable terms," I told Sheila. "He wasn't asserting..."

The music rose higher, drowning my voice.

Sheila was watching Sophie and J.C.M. Joe lose themselves into each other's embrace.

Much later the music changed to a more rapid flow in rhythm. Sophie and J.C.M. Joe flew around the hall in colours like two butterflies on a honeymoon. They then came and joined us near the hissing cymbals and heart-thumping drums.

"Enjoying yourselves?" asked Sophie when the music ceased.

"Oh yes – quite, Sophie," answered Sheila.

"How is it, brother?" asked J.C.M. Joe.

"Same as yesterday, last year and the years before," I answered, not expecting anyone to hear me.

A second year student came up and asked me if he could dance with Sheila.

"Ask her."

Sophie pulled me out to the center of the hall for a dance and I left after that.

I strolled outside, leaving all to the shadowy crimson of the hall, to get myself blanketed into the nocturnal silence that remained towered by concrete buildings. In the darkness I imagined myself to be Count Dracula and smiled with mirthful content. A few girls and boys stood smoking cigarettes, drinking lolly water and generally chatting and giggling callowly while leaning against the thick cement railings. How ironical it is, I thought, to have people preaching against darkness at broad daylight then retreat to the normal "sins" of the night like this.

"I suppose I shall have to follow you since Joseph took all the trouble pairing us off tonight." It was Sheila speaking out of the dark from behind me. I didn't expect her to follow and thinking this was absurd for her, I laughed carelessly, but kept walking.

"What is funny?"

"Nothing. I was just wondering if J.C.M. Joe had made a mistake of pairing me off with a high school kid."

Sheila let out a gutsy utter of scorn but kept following me. At the door of our room I turned and asked if she wanted to come in. She just shrugged, opened the door herself and turned the light on. She sat on my bed, shrugged again, and stared at me.

"Hellow," I smiled, eyeing her full on the face.

She was shy all of a sudden. Looking down at the floor, she said, "It is funny—I don't know why I—I keep thinking of you... Really, honestly, brother, I—I just cannot help it—but I just cannot keep you out of my mind." She took in a little pause for granted, then giggled. "I hope you are not using any love magic on me." and at the words 'love magic' Sheila looked up to me; her face suddenly turned sour. I went and sat beside her, uneasily. She remained still.

"But I am so ordinary," I told her, almost painfully.

She rose and turned the main light off after turning on J.C.M. Joe's shady study light.

"People might look in and see us," she explained nervously.

The room was now semi-lighted and I imagined Sheila felt comfortable in it. She came and sat beside me. I looked at the floor. Minutes ticked by. Faint and distant echoes of the electric guitars made only soft twangings in our ears, and I thought, this Sheila is trapped. The word 'trapped' shook me by surprise, making me want to hold Sheila out of an urgency I could not define. I rose, moved to open the door for her, but then I stopped and turned.

Her body felt soft and cool as she rose to accept my embrace. Her breath from those tiny nostrils rushed gale-like at my neck in fine streamlines of unperturbed gusts. We kissed. Quite naturally. Her mouth, her flesh, tasted like green coconut meat.

I felt, in this embrace, that I was painting in La, a three dimensional self-portrait; one part of me wanted to push her away and tell her to get the hell out of my life; the other just simply groaned, 'I'll make love to you, I'll make love to you, I'll make love to you;' while the third remained calmed of my senses, numb and was wishing time to stand still. It was the third that finally overwhelmed me, captured the stilled moment for itself, saving my soul, enabling me to hold La tighter.

"Bro—brother?" she squealed, the word wriggled its way out of her mouth.

"Mm?" the third part of me responded.

"Is—is this what your first and heart-warming hullo meant to mean when you looked at me full on the face for the first time and in this room?"

All the three parts of me remained silent. More minutes ticked by, leaving Sheila and I stranded in unity, in a deserted room of loneliness and *lusmanship*.

Then the first and second part of me retorted her question, "Was it my topping of the class in H.S.T. that made you want to talk to me? Or is it what you think I am that...?"

"No, please do not be a fool," she said, burying her head under my chin. "It is you, you. I—I just... want... you...". Sheila then held me tighter. "But why, why, why?" she complained. "Why must you be so persistently evasive? Why must you be so painstakingly indifferent? Will you not let yourself out for the others? You do not give them much choice—*weu, alou...* " She winced then employed another *'alou'* which I had guessed was an expression of motherly grace in her language. I wondered what Mary would think if she saw me with Sheila; probably raise an authorative finger of "Do not joke on the family. Multiply it."

In the semi-lighted room I felt all of my three characters melt to merge into a single being: nothing. That embrace then became a revival of that unconscious part of me that was Mary; that was Enita; that was Anuki; that was the father I have never known nor met—an extension to the world I had created through dreams and fantasies right from All Saints' to my prelim at the University. And that extension was what the present world would regard as nothingness. My nothingness. And if ever the world outside, the material bourgeois world of luxury and glorious achievements, caught me with Sheila and raised a finger of accusation, shouting, "Hey you there. What is this nothingness that you preach of? Speak, you unproductive bludger", then my only shouts of ricochet would have been, "You. Your absence. The absence of your present meanings. *That* is my Nothingness."

Further, however, that embrace alone became an exotic world that absorbed me, and the physical part of me that held La became nil, transmitting its senses to the other part of me which was entirely human, spiritual and most important of all, emotional, through which I was seeing the girl as a pebble of nakedness before me. "I have to be emotional," the latter part of me reflected; "to disregard emotions, to brush them off and partially prefer the physical and intellectual parts of my being to the rest of me, will mean my denying the fact that I am human... And now, of all my life, this is the ultimate, still full of determination yet never reaching a decision, never wanting to embrace a moment I can accept as an highest point for the self-esteem, my satisfaction. So holding you, Sheila Jivi La, what is there to utter but to be simply calmed, to be granted peace and sacred silence that neither lives nor dies, neither saves nor destroys, neither speaks nor remains sullen, but becomes one single moment of impartial human emotion, to be. The whole world, I understand, will shout out my name for shame, for guilt, for fornication... yet how else must I reclaim a fated being?"

"No, no, no," Sheila was screaming hysterically. Yet when I returned to the world of reality, her reality, I could only hear her urging me to stop what I was doing. "Darling, please... no..." was now her own pleading voice, with I just animatedly sighing, "Hey, this is good. It feels so good..."

She pushed me away.

The next moments that followed were of silent retreats into our own selves, feeling the guilt of having broken into each other's life.

"My father is a Priest," Sheila spoke suddenly and firmly, as if accusing me of a wrong. "I am a Christian." She sat on my bed and placed her arms between her closed thighs as if in defence.

"We both are Christians," I said, with my arms outstretched, resembling a crucifix.

She looked up, "No, that is not what I mean—"

"Well, what do you mean then?"

"I am just saying that it is not right for me—for us—if we do what you wanted us to do a minute ago." She paused, fumbling for words. "I—I mean, it is quite all right, but it must wait. We – we shall have to finish our degrees first."

"By that time, I'll be dead," I thought.

"Tell me, have you ever heard of anything like beauty in youth, beauty in life, purgation in love—?"

"Please, do not try to talk me into it—"

"You are scared, Sheila."

"Aren't you? I mean, you are a boy so it is quite all right with you. The whole world is yours; you can do whatever you wish. But aren't you, in anyway at all, scared?"

"Of being pregnant—?"

"No – of impurities – of sin –"

"I have no sins, La," I said.

"You cannot have no sins," argued Sheila, still in her careful English, and showing a face of both contempt and incredulity."This is ridiculous. No human being is all pure, do you see the sense in that – do you understand?"

"No," I sighed helplessly. "When I said I had no sins, I meant my own world of innocence that negates your definition of sin."

Sheila thought for a moment then giggled. Rather, it was a bitter laugh from out of her soul that was in strife.

She said, "Really, honestly, I feel guilty about this—I mean, what you tried to do with me."

I thought, "If I forced my way into you, Sheila Jivi La, you would be saying something else different."

"I feel wronged," continued Sheila, "I feel utterly wounded. Really... all this time I have been thinking that you were a quiet, decent person, but your behaviour .. it frightens me."

She shrugged. A moment of silence hung in the air above and between us. Then slowly she said, "I suppose it is something I have grown up with—to speak sensibly enough, I mean. Well, just like you regarding the wrong itself, the perverse silence, as something of a deep respect. It is the same with me, my father is a Priest in the Church, my life is of the Church and there is no way I can rebel. So we more or less have the same amount of persistence in us but for different reasons." She was speaking to the floor.

But she looked up suddenly, alarmed. "It is not my fault, is it?—if I think this way?"

I was silently observing her.

"I said, it is not my fault, is it?"

"No."

She got up from the bed, walked past me to the door, but changed her mind, stopped where she was and, slowly turning around, she shrugged, "It is useless. We both cannot—"She stopped there. Her face remained expressionless for a moment, then she looked at the greyed ceiling, blinking two or three times out of deep thinking. J.C.M. Joe and I had not swept the room, I noticed.

Later, and to my surprise, Sheila Jivi La walked up to me, smiling confidently. She fastened her arms around me when I let her, and we remained thus for a long time. She now looked at my face without fear, gently releasing her grip only to cup my face in her little hands, to give me a long passionate kiss that gave us both the feeling of belonging to some common agreement. And at that moment I remembered Jimi Damebo's poetry and almost shed tears, fragments, in fact, of my soul on the concrete floor beneath us.

Sheila then whispered, "But I am not afraid of you. You are weak—you would not hurt an innocent ant."

"Whatever do you mean by that, La?" I asked in alarm. Sheila laughed aloud, threw herself at me again, then said, "What is there that I must fear about you? Your indifference, your silence, your dislike for the presence of other people around you, do not scare me anymore. Hah, I am no longer scared, like the day I walked up to you and congratulated you for topping the class in HST and—and all I got was a weird, monstrous stare from you. I."

"Good-bye, La," I spoke firmly, but calmly uncoiling her arms from my seventeen year-old physique.

I had passed my exams well, with distinctions in most of the subjects. Mary had not written since I wrote her. Father Jefferson had written a six-page letter accusing me of turning away from the Church, of being involved in politics when I had "absolutely no business whatsoever", etc., Mr Goldsworth too, although living not far from the campus, wrote me a take-it-easy letter. Which meant that there was no one to write to about my academic efforts.

I forgot or ignored La and I communicated with Just Call Me Joe only through the essays he had asked me to write for the Black Power Movement columns in *'Nilaidat'* or for his forums. Yet at most times the movement received little response from me in terms of participation; each time I was asked to chair a forum or write a few paragraphs for an Australian university newsletter, I would struggle to think up an excuse not to be involved—irrespective of how many times I had been accused by Just Call Me Joe and the senior student politicians of 'attempting to be a traitor' or 'failing to observe the brotherhood concern for the import, the survival and the success of the Movement'.

For most part of the year everything had turned out worse for me. Once at a beer party in one of the professors' residences a senior Black Power member punched me for making statements that were 'proved contradictory' to the movement's 'well-thought out policies'. I left everyone else out of my mind after that, occasionally spending two or three agonizing nights away from the room, never turning up for lectures and tutorials the following days.

And besides, what would be more consoling than to flee the imprisonment of academic horrors and confusion, just to learn the art of getting drunk with *wantoks* on my five dollars in town then to return to the silent room to be hailed a hero by its emptiness, Che and the near-nude?

Upon one broad daylight I fell out of a fast moving bus at Hohola. I was not the least surprised. What could a centless, discontented village mope do but deliberately fall out after five miles of free ride, merrily claiming that, "it is part of my life, *wantok,*" much to the annoyance of the yawning black-toothed bus driver, the sweating loyal Black Jack the law *lusman* in blue, and the passersby who flocked about me? In the red-eyed, betel-blood mouthed, Mekeo-hairdone Hohola dwellers who came to witness my fall, I had no pride; no confiding refuge; not even innate prime—yet I was one of them. And to the mysterious unknown piously hidden behind miles of clear blue sky above, I showed my bruised knees and elbows then spat; "Look at me, Ozymandias - Big Boss. Look at me. Look at my bruised knees and elbows. Look at my wounded soul. I am your creation, ah? And who is there in the world that must look upon your work and despair?"

Then all around me I could just make out sighs of disgust from men, calls of disdain from women, giggles of mockery from school girls out for lunch, inviting laughs from worn-out betel-nut sellers, while simultaneously being sliced by the blazing whips of heat that came down from the burning fireball above me.

I walked.

Vehicles of sorts raided the Waigani Road that day, raising twirls of thick dust in the air for my lungs to devour. But were those vehicles driven in a straight line? I thought, always consistent to a particular pattern and direction, at a set speed, by happy-go-lucky blind fools. None of the drivers had the initiative enough to make a victorious turn to the nearest bush to crash or be free of traffic rules. And of those in the vehicles, they were black, brown, yellow, coffee-coloured and white faces; white faces roaring hungrily down the highway in expensive sports cars after the hard-exploited profits that awaited them somewhere in the city; yellow men screeching past them in creamy white Toyotas, so superior, so rich, so industrious, to sell scones and lolly water to the natives in the dusty parts of Moresby's newly erected settlements; black faces in enormous lorries grinding up and down the highway again and again to load, unload, to re-load, unre-load the wiry, soiled-fuzzyhaired, sweat-shiny black and brown huddled clumps of humanity that had never had the time to spare for breakfast and lunch in years; white men driving brand new Datsuns and Mercedes with their black girls who jutted their elbows out of the windows and giggled at the *lusman* on the roadside; white women behind wheels and brakes of second-hand junk with their black men who sat contemplating what destiny there was withheld for them; and in that buzzing excitement and nerve-snapping heat a mirage of nostalgia formed far ahead of me: from the bushes popped dogcollared, black-cloaked, baldheaded moralists to hail the people in the vehicles, "Stop! Stop, you fools. Stop and turn—this the way, this is the way"; yet it was useless for the Church elders; they had only to cough chokingly in the dust left by the stubborn, metallic statues behind the steering wheels. The highway then became one long assembly of a huge factory of humans, all being manufactured, shaped, moulded by the very vehicles they drove. It would be far from the set rules of that huge factory if anyone of the drivers stopped to offer me a lift. 'The rules are there to determine our motion which must always be forward', I once heard a public servant explain.

At Tokarara Junction the traffic eased down to two or three at intervals of one or two minutes. Drivers were now yawning as they hissed past and I imagined the lunch rush hour was over.

I came across a group of girls who seemed to have nothing better to spend their day in than to call out to each other in *tok ples,* to let out seductive whistles as if deliberately trying to catch my attention or jokingly shout to the male drivers for 'twenty dollar one drop only'. They were dusty and crowned by wiry, uncombed knotted hair and wearing what should have been once bright floral dresses, now appeared as loose calico clothing heavily greyed by the seasons of urban blind conformity. They were, of course, the daughters of the soil, squandering the joys of youth to the dirtiest full, after being washed from their villages to the city like drifting seaside coconuts by the inevitable tide of random migration. They continued finger-whistling and letting out bubbles of sensuous laughter as I came nearer; I crossed the road to avoid them.

"Hey bro," one of them, a smaller girl, shouted after me across the road. "You want this girl?" she asked, giggled, then pointed to the biggest girl among them. "She my sister. She want you."

"Ah, *faita larefa* cup of coffee—*koi koi,* " I shouted back, testily.

"*Ia* true, bro. We not tricking you. She want you."

"Yes, we all of us wants you," joined in the rest.

"Hey my bro, this one for you," yelled the smaller girl, letting her hips twirl with childish rudeness. An excited explosion of merriment swayed the heads of the group, like a breeze of freedom in human existence gushing at a small cluster of leaves.

"*Ia* bro," they called and laughed. "You very handsome. But how you learn our language, bro? You spoke it fine. Just fine." (Wild and excited yappings followed.)

"Hey bro, you too small." (One girl's voice.) "Aha. Me, I will make you cry for your Mama's susu. Aha ha ha, oh *Dirava."* (More laughter and excited calls in *tok pies.)*

"But how you know our language, bro?"(All.) "You mix race, ah? Ah bro, bro, anytime."

They were getting closer. They reminisced no one in particular in the past seventeen years of my experiences of just existing; yet their presence etched a spark of hope, of the sense of belonging in me, of even the understanding of the sensuality I had inherited from an anonymous father and perhaps Enita and Mary too, and that spark of hope was the realisation of the fact that we, the girls on the road and I, were mere pebbles of *lusman-tasol,* custom-stripped village idiots whose virginity had been deprived through urban nets of confusion, no longer fearing the world that surround us, no longer wanting, no longer yearning for ways to compensate the traditional rules we had overlooked, we had disregarded, we had fowned upon even through beers tears, just to come to be in the city; no, not even remembering to question the meaning of this alien life to which we were plunged by time, by our own youthful desires, for new and exciting ventures. Then, how could we win.

"Hey bro. We really wants you. True, honest to *Divara* we does."

"Ah, bro—you how."

Very few cars whizzed past. High above me, as usual for Moresby's weather, black clouds were swelling for an afternoon's rainstorm. Yet those clouds would be swept away by the southern winds to the remote regions somewhere in the Highlands, leaving Moresby to her own wealth of dust, menacing Tokarara red soil, clean devastation through bulldozers of social change and urbanisation, and the 'one way' necessity for general national development. Those squalid girls and I, somehow, constituted that destruction out of some vague loyalty to a principle, or belief, or even custom-substituted conformity to the leftovers of human development, that destined us not to travel by buses, PMV's, taxis, luxurious cars, etc, but to bare-footedly tread the hard gravel and partly tarred soil of our country's capital city. We were the waste on the roadside for someone else's long, bitumen highway, always flowing forward to civilisation.

Sweat soaked me, my feet were dusty and tired, and I was panting like a dog when I reached the campus. I went to the Mess to see if it was still open. I was late for lunch. All around me there was a hustle of hurrying students, wearing the usual faces of professional studentship, books resting in their homely places of underarms, all going in one direction. Very few mumurrings could be heard. I followed the students, more out of curiosity than of interest, to ask one what the hurry was for. I could not get near enough to do so. A student in one of the tutorial rooms just before the library and the foyer of the students' forum carelessly let out a full blast of music from a transistor thus drawing attention from the frozen faces who sneered, scrutinised the student out of annoyance and later silenced him by a chorus of angry shouts. Guilt forced the careless student, who was enjoying the music, to quickly turn off the transistor and bite a finger with fear and childish embarrassment. He stood up slowly, as soon as he was ignored, and went and joined the crowd at the forum. Then I learnt what the silent commotion was about; I had accidently arrived in time for one of the Black Power Movement's forums, with Just Call Me Joe just walking into the arena to introduce the speakers.

The crowd was at its climax of a thousand or two, most of it spread along the cement stairs that fell to the floor of the forum, and still a pack of it peering at the arena from above the library, the cement railing of the Union Hall and the roof of the Main Lecture Theatre. I was wondering what the topic of the forum was until a large and long strip of canvas, on which giant inscriptions in red were conspicuous and which was suspended just above the arena of the forum supported by strings that were tied to the rails of the library and the Union Hall, caught my eye. The huge inscription was a quote from a speech I had prepared for Just Call Me Joe a few weeks back, all of it written down as it was, its truth and implications, its bluff and protests, its parody and contradictions, left untouched by any member of the Black Power Movement. I was glad but scared at the same time; while the crowd cheered, jeered, boohooed and cried about the inscription, while one just stood by and shuddered at every empathetical word from Just Call Me Joe and the senior student politicians because one was white, while one felt one's heart thud with guilt, with anger, because one was married to an Australian, while one was a New Guinean racist in reverse, while one was a Christian whose moral beliefs must not be balked, while one was an atheist because everyone else was or because one was scared of the Holy *Dirava* Himself, while that student with the transistor sat hidden in an ear-phone letting his fingers and studentship awareness escape into the rhythm of whatever music he was listening to, while yet others held clenched fists in the air or employed brutal drives of folded newspapers into the hard brick walls, I felt my hopes and emotions melt to merge into a single pool of horror out of possible self-betrayal; in preparing that last speech for Just Call Me Joe, I had abandoned the idea of just advocating that 'the Black Man must live.' The crowd then was only roaring at my being which I had butchered to shreds for Just Call Me Joe and the other Black Power members to display for all to see:

WE ALL ARE VICTIMS
CAUGHT IN THE NETS OF WHITE MAN'S MATERIAL
ACHIEVEMENTS AND FRUSTRATIONS. OUR
ENDEAVOUR IS TO BREAK DOWN THOSE
ACHIEVEMENTS AND FRUSTRATIONS IN ORDER TO
SAVE THAT MAN, THAT WHOLESOME BLACK

INDIVIDUAL, WHO WILL IN TURN CONSTITUTE
AN ENLIGHTENED NATION.

The forum ended. The crowd walked away in all directions, exchanging grins of satisfaction, with the exception of a good few who swarmed Just Call Me Joe and the senior student politicians to either pretentiously congratulate them or argue with them on any point that was vague. Just Call Me Joe smiled and shook hands with some of them, mostly whites who showed signs of understanding his studentship political aspirations.

I walked away.

I wandered around the campus, killing time before I could return to the room to sleep the afternoon away. Few students roamed about the academic buildings, but most were stealing off to the city to probably do some shopping or get drunk on their five dollars. (I had spent all my scholarship wealth the day before, when learning to be a dignified drunkard as well as a superior human chimney; I preferred the former, although J.C.M. Joe had succeeded in convincing me to take up smoking. 'It feels luxurious, you know," he had explained.) The afternoon air felt cool, as I wasted my study time on the green grass that linked each solid concrete building. The sky above me became darkened as if promising that the rain clouds were there to stay. I was lying on my back just outside the library and opposite the forum, with my legs spread, as I leisured this sudden change of weather. Today, I thought, it will rain, and the rain will bring with it the fresh reminiscences of Enita, of Mary, of the sea of solitude, of Yaguyawa-Kuburina, of...

Just Call Me Joe and I were in the room when it poured, with its lightning and distant thunder rumbling silently at the dumb Arts/Law building and the Main Lecture Theatre which resembled huge obscure forms of elephants in deep indifferent slumber. The room, since we last cleaned it over a hundred years ago, was again dank, unswept and too cool. One would feel one was living in a cold country now that the rain had come again to the customarily dry surroundings of Port Moresby. The cold wind whistled past us just outside. It might have been too cool but to me the cold breath of that rain-storm brought laughter, life. I began, however, feeling depressed again after discovering that my sudden happiness was meant for no one. Only Just Call Me Joe moved about the room at ease as usual for the academic enthusiast, with that bright personality he'd always displayed, like a fluttering butterfly in his newly adopted Afro-Asian cloak which I saw him wearing at the forum. The cloak was too loose, oversized—it must have been one of the Political Science tutor's—like a woman's nightgown. Still, Just Call Me Joe danced the floor of the room in it, kicked my chair, tipped our bin full of paper waste which scattered all over thus aggravating the unswept atmosphere around us, and from his study desk he knocked off an ash tray which shattered on the floor.

He did not notice.

"I'm going to Canberra," he said instead, surprising me.

I eyed him full on the face: "Oh? When, J.C.M. Joe?"

"Why, after graduation, of course," he laughed.

"Well, congrats.—" I extended my hand; he didn't take it; he was still dancing the floor of the untidy room.

"I'm going to Sydney," he laughed again. "I'm going to Melbourne, Adelaide, Ottawa, Japan, England, Ohio Express, Nigeria, Phillippines—"

"Ohio Express, did you say?" I interrupted, wondering if there was such a place.

"Oh yes—Ohio Express, Texas, New Delhi, Dodge City, Singapore, Santa Cruz, Rome, New York, Irian Barat, Warandyte, Goroka, Nazareth, Pumani, oh, all over the world."

"Amazing," I thought.

"And where was Sheila Jivi La going?" I wondered. I found myself regretting I would miss her hullos and light hugs too— something, I admit, I expected most of Sheila from deep inside. Perhaps she would go back to her Mission Station where her father was a Priest and do some welfare work. Sheila would do well as a community developer while J.C.M. Joe would be a diplomat telling the world that I, the *lusman,* was satisfied with everything in my country. And in the wonder alone of what everyone would become I cursed myself quietly at the thought of having to be included as one of the worldly products from the Goldsworth factory of All Saints'. I thought of those others who were now scattered all over the Territory; I wondered what James St. Nativeson was up to and where he was; what was Nathaniel working as?—probably both working as clerks, rotting away somewhere in the confinement of bureaucratic enclosures and they could even be in Moresby now. And what about that fool who said that I was a double-skinned fatherless bastard at Posa Bay? And of that student with his transistor radio?

I felt comfortable when J.C.M. Joe ceased dancing in the room. I lay on my bed, wanting to shut him out. Or at least let my mind be healed by the hssing rain outside, which would also help me sleep the afternoon away. But he rose again, this time rehearsing a speech he would give to an audience at Monash University – about the whole country and having all Papua New Guineans reassert themselves and face the world without shame, and for Christ's sake go get the false rumour that we had once been head-hunters and cannibals. He then went to the dirty mirror, brushed his wiry hair with his palms, admired the way he sucked at the cigarette, smiled, then turned to me. I had my eyes opened in time to watch all these movements.

I sat up straight on my bed. I felt my eye-lids narrow, silently observing Just Call Me Joe. I was leaning against the colour blowup of Che.

"Hey," he exclaimed suddenly, calling my names. "Why are you staring at me that way?"

I felt my body shudder when Just Call Me Joe called me by my surname; the name which I had erased together with the others in my birth certificate simply because it proclaimed the promise that I too, happily, had a father.

"Brother? Anything wrong?"

"Nothing, J.C.M. Joe. I think it's the cold wind from the rain that is giving me the chills."

"Come off it, man. There must be something wrong. Not Sheila?"

"No, not Sheila," I said, no longer pretending.

"Then what in the arsehole is the matter with you?" He was furious.

"I am beginning to be afraid, Joseph."

"Afraid?" He went and sat on his bed. "Afraid of what?"

"Of my brothers – of my sisters – of – of – "

"Shit," he laughed aloud, throwing his head back. He then sat up erect, majestic in his Afro-Asian cloak, looking superior like Goldsworth, but more like a William Dobell portrait staring through his nostrils at me. He said, "What a piece of philosophy to make. Did it take you the whole year to think it out? Ha, *aiaka*. Who am I listening to?"

He shot up to his feet, looking more superior than ever. His hands were clutched at his back, his head held high just to ignore the near-nude then went and sat down again, gracefully, on his bed. He crossed his legs and lit a cigarette with as much feminity as a woman I saw at Goldsworth's dinner party. How does he do it? I asked myself out of alarm. Where did all these luxurious cloaks, fancy gestures and money come from? But my silent quests were answered easily when he threw down a magazine on my side of the floor and told me to look through it. I did, and to my dismay—almost self-pity—I found a photograph of him with a clenched fist, and a column of printing under it whose words, apart from the caption, were definitely mine.

"Where were the royalties?" I wondered.

"See what I mean?" he said, proudly pointing to the article. "I mean, what is there to be afraid of? The world outside has at last opened its ears to listen to us. What is there to fear? We're in business, aren't we?"

"Yes, J.C.M. Joe," I agreed, thinking, 'a social derelict,' and at the same time frightened by the thought.

Just Call Me Joe snapped his fingers, motioning me to follow him meekly outside. The rain still poured. With his Afro-Asian cloak looking too monstrous to be colourful, I felt I could in no way ask J.C.M. Joe to slow down, to turn around and have a second look at me, before proceeding further on the road to freedom. Still, he watched the rain with satisfaction; and with his hands authoratively buried into the pockets of his cloak, he looked a 'Big Man'. I was chilled then.

We both stood watching the rain, but blanketed by our own thoughts.

Far up the bitumen street that led to the now-misted Main Lecture Theatre and the adjoining buildings a group of students emerged, playing ball in the thick rain. They played down the street until they reached the patch of green below us. The girls ran after the boys who had the ball, to squeeze it away from them, and vice versa, and I soon recognised Sheila Jivi La among them. She snatched the ball from one of the boys and ran towards us only to chuck it at J.C.M. Joe who caught the ball gracefully then smiled down paternally.

"Come on down and enjoy the rain," shouted Sheila from below.

"Come on, you two. You cannot miss such good fun."

The other students, all in shorts, urged us with the same words.

J.C.M. Joe assured them he would, after throwing back the ball to Sheila. Then he started tip-toeing, partly winging like a bird with his hands, swaying in the air, down the stairs.

"Come on, *tevera,*" shouted Sheila. She kissed the ball then threw it back to me.

"Come on, La," the others shouted, "Stop fooling around with the ball. Just go up and drag him down, or kiss him, or rape him, or do anything—as long as we have the ball back."

I caught the ball with difficulty, thinking, 'I need some exercise'. I kissed it then threw it back, feeling it was my duty to do so. Sheila smiled, urging me to go down to her. But before she could feel any response from me, Just Call Me Joe rushed out from under the building, grabbed both Sheila and the ball, then charged at the waiting little crowd. They all played in a ring of mutual harmony and happiness. The boys cheered and clapped with their heads tilted back, tongues out to suck the rain, while the girls shouted or giggled then fell onto the grass to roll over and over. Sheila was lost in that little crowd.

Dusk came as a blessing, after the rain. It was cool, safe, and had inked in me a lot of satisfying reminiscences, like birth, like peace, like waiting for dawn—I indulged in waiting—and my mind silently surrendered to its dying serenity. I stood facing the sunset just outside the Mess, unconscious of the hurrying students around me who were anxious to get their feed before nightfall. I had made up my mind; I wanted to go and tell Just Call Me Joe everything.

He was in the room, now darkened by the retiring light of the dusk, tapping away at a typewriter which he had borrowed from the English Department. He forgot to put the light on. What's he typing? I asked myself, thinking, when one runs out of ideas typewriters are used as shields to defend oneself against the suspicious world. I entered quietly, feeling confident and whole.

"Ahem," I said.

Just Call Me Joe kept typing.

"Ahem," I said again. He stopped, only to swear at the typewriter, then continued.

I coughed for the third time then noisily shut the door, feeling a bubble of mocking laughter well up in me. He looked up, but did not see me; he was looking, for the first time, at the dying light that meagred through the hole he had punched on our door at the beginning of the first semester.

"I want to talk to you, Just Call Me Joe," I spoke to the dark form of him, which remained motionless on his study chair.

After a brief silence he changed the direction of his gaze, this time towards my face, then shrugged in the semi-darkness.

"What about?" he asked a little later, in a tone which indicated that we were no longer friends.

"I want to talk to you, Just Call Me Joe... as a friend."

"What—after all these months of dumb silence from you? *Ehe.*"

"I want you to listen to me, Just Call Me Joe," I shouted and simultaneously switched on the light. He blinked a few times, but quickly recovered to let his dimples curve deeper into a mocking smile.

"Tch-tch-tch, violence, violence—slow down, brother," he clucked the pretentious condoling tones as if supporting that mocking smile. "Slow down, slow down, kid. It's only me, Joseph, your brother."

"You are even forgetting your name, Joseph," I was standing stiff and staring at the ceiling when I said this.

He did not move. He stopped smiling too. He got the message. I was not joking.

He withdrew to his bed, lay on his back and, gazing at the slow revolving fan and the ceiling, said, "What is it, brother?"

"I'm leaving uni."

"You are what?" he sat up abruptly on his bed.

"I'm getting a job."

Just Call Me Joe rose slowly to face me, his eyes blazing out of sheer shock. I had never seen him so serious and concerned before.

"Brother," he exclaimed, his lips and cheeks quivering with horror. "You'll kill yourself. The people who constitute the whole of the public service are absolute shits and you'll die being with them."

"I know. That's why I'm leaving."

"But that's suicide."

"What have I got to lose?" I shrugged.

"A lot, brother. A lot. I mean, being a student is so tormenting and pays very little but that's the only chance for us all."

"What's so special about being a student?" I quoted someone I had overheard somewhere.

He just stared at me, unbelieving. Then he pushed his head forward, gripped me powerfully by the shoulders, and asked with deliberate care, "Tell me, brother, what exactly are you after?"

I laughed aloud, formed my hands into two little balls of fists, then gave him my whole weight of two forceful punches; one on his nose, the other against his chest with an enormous thud. He reeled back, stunned. Blood jetted from his nostrils. I was still laughing. He shook his head frantically, then joined me in a wild roar of manic laughter, wiping his bleeding nose with his fingers. He stood back then charged at me with bigger and stronger fists swinging in the air, but stopped short to let his arms fall, to be immediately followed by his brief and careless shrug. He punched another hole on our thick wooden door instead and said, "I am sorry, brother, for everything."

"That's okay, J.C.M. Joe," I returned, grinning. "I just want you to know that you are the only one in the world I regard as a brother." I walked up to him again and landed six more blows to which J.C.M. Joe showed no resistance, until my knuckles hurt. Then I employed brutal kicks to his body to prove my mix-blooded manhood; around his ribs, to his face; continuous and vicious thuds from my foot landed on his chest as soon as he lay on the floor until I retreated when I felt my own body ache. I picked up my study chair, weighed it in the air and was about to hurl it at him when he raised his hand for peace.

"Thank you, sir," I smiled, and put down the chair.

He only laughed. It was, as before, a bitter laugh.

He went to the mirror to examine his battered face.

"This is the only victory I have ever seen in all my life," I sighed. "And I deserve that victory."

"I wish you did," sighed J.C.M. Joe. "You know, I could have killed you, brother," he then added, grinning at his own reflection in the mirror. "Your head's too bloody small, I don't know what would be left of it after my first punch. Ha, a*ia goude.*" But there was a trembling tone of sadness in his voice when he had said this, and to my surprise he was already weeping uncontrollably while leaning against the mirror. "Don't worry about me," he was now saying; "I'll trudge along."

I started packing my things, simultaneously numb about J.C.M. Joe's presence. Towards half-past seven that evening he felt better while lying on his bed, but this time letting his mind lose itself on the funny patterns that decorated the ceiling. I finished packing all my belongings, except the bed sheets and the pillow cases which belonged to the future occupants of the room. I sat at my desk meaning to write a letter to someone, but thinking of none, I just drew and scribbled on the pad anything that came into my mind, until the name Enita appeared. Then I drew a tear, with Mary's eye in it. I drew a smile under the tear. It was Sophie's. What about Sheila? That's ridiculous. She's barely a hundred yards away. I turned suddenly to Just Call Me Joe.

"Hey J.C.M. Joe," I said. "I'm trying to write a letter to anyone in the world. Any ideas?"

"Write to Father Jefferson."

"Oh."

A heavy hand rested on my shoulder as I was saying good-bye to Father Jefferson in the letter. Just Call Me Joe was peering down at me.

"May I say something, brother?'

"What?"

"Please go and see Sheila."

"I will, J.C.M. Joe. For your sake."

"No," he said, slowly, carefully. "It's not for my sake, brother. You kids just don't realize how much you need each other. Hell, kids. Don't jus die."

He was sobbing again.

I rose without a word and walked out leaving Father Jefferson's letter to the care fo Just Call Me Joe.

Serenity hung on a rigging all around me, and the hot air left by the now-dead-gone sun on the bitumen street that ran past the girls' dormitory rose to infatuate my nose. Dusk, I noticed, had completely died out on me.

A Tolai student, in a pair of white trunks and a red T-shirt with the insignia 'One Way Jesus', stood at the door of the girls' dormitory, picking her finger nails which were painted green.

"I see Sheila, please?" I asked her.

"It's past visiting hours," she said.

"It's a quarter to eight," I returned, seriously.

"She's not in," she teased her green finger nails.

"I want to talk to Sheila, please," I raised my voice a little.

"Why don't you sign yourself in?" she asked.

"No, you bring her out."

She looked at me through half-raised brows of surprise. I wanted to let her know that I had never quarrelled with girls before and I did not want to be forced to either; but fearing her brothers would be around somewhere, I decided not to. She turned and, over her shoulder, remarked, "The Lord be praised." I was wondering what her Lord was being praised for.

Sheila came out a few minutes later with a towel wrapped around her.

"What is wrong?" she asked.

"I want to talk to you."

"Sure, " she said, and walked towards me with one hand supporting the towel, the other combing through her wet hair.

"No, Sheila," I said. "I want to really talk to you."

"Well, you are now, aren't you? she said, and spun her hair to let the water run off. A few drops showered my face. She had just come out of the womb.

"What I mean is for you to go in and get dressed. It's important that I talk to you—alone."

A male securityguard came out to the door, pretending not to listen to us.

Sheila stared at me for some time, then disappeared into the dormitory without protest. It took her half-an-hour to get dressed, or so my impatience told me, and when she finally emerged from the building, she complained that her clothes from the day's laundry were not thoroughly dry. She then rushed down the brief stairs and, throwing her body all around me, said, "What is the conference about, Dadi?"

"Hey, hey, hey, where did you get this 'Dadi' from?"

"From the way you talk, the way you walk, the way you appear in my nightly dreams and they are all sweet dreams."

"Oh dear", I thought, and looked around to see if the security guard was still there. He had disappeard. I smelt perfume.

"Let's go to my room," I suggested quickly.

She obeyed, but asked, "Is Joseph in?"

"Yes."

"That's good, because I don't trust you," she said and, hugging me, added, "After graduation, Big Boy, all Sheila Jivi La will be yours and yours truly."

Promises, promises, promises; when kids make promises they are nothing but promises.

"Oh by the way," said Sheila, "my father wrote me yesterday."

"Oh. How are they?"

"All well. I told them about you in the last letter."

"What do they think?"

"Mother said it is quite all right if we are friends, but she would like me to finish my course first. Father sounded just vague in the letter." She laughed, then said, "Oh, my dear father. He is so worried about a whole lot of things."

"Did you tell them that I'm..."

"We are Christians, brother. Please understand that."

"Christians or not, whatever your parents say must be taken into account, Sheila."

"Sometimes they may be wrong, you know."

"Well, yes," I said, thinking of Enita. "But they must be respected, anyway."

"I also told them you went to All Saints'."

"Oh? What does Father Gabriel think of the old school?"

"He thinks highly of it. He is even sending Paul there next year."

"Who's Paul?"

"My small brother." Then she added, "Also your brother-in-law," after which she bit my right ear. She then wheeled me around to face her. "And brother, please do not be afraid. I am sure they will accept you as their son-in-law." Some students walking past heard Sheila and giggled in the semi-darkness. My heart laughed with them, but I quickly held her not wanting the pretence to be detected.

"Iei, ita i rage," she called out to the giggling students. *"Auou ita baiei.* Blasted unsophisticated *pamuks."*

"Sheila," I said, feeling alarm for her. "Watch your language."

"Sorry, Dadi," she returned, still agitated and calling out abuses after the students. We shall all be butchered and raped by heterosexual homosexuals, was what the anger in Sheila Jivi La meant. I wondered if she knew that.

In the room J.C.M. Joe looked up slowly from the typewriter but after seeing Sheila he shot up in joy.

"Hullo, hullo, my sister," he greeted her, cupping her face in his hands. "How may you be?"

He gave her forehead a light brush with his lips in the Western tradition. Sheila just smiled pleasantly and told him she was well.

"Sit down, sit down, sister," he said, pushing his study chair forward. "Well, how are you finding this Anuki *doga?* Pretty complicated, isn't he?"

"Not tonight, Joseph," said Sheila, seating her little body on the chair. "Tonight was the only time he brought himself down to earth to speak to me."

"I can see that," said J.C.M. Joe.

Then Sheila noticing Just Call Me Joe's face, exclaimed, "Joseph. What happened to your face?"

J.C.M. Joe laughed, then smiled tenderly, "Well you see, my sister, I was going up a ladder, trying to reach heaven or some such place, which was beautiful anyway, I thought; then someone removed the footing of the ladder, you see, so I couldn't just refuse to fall, could I? Anyway, I fell, battered my face on the cement floor but here I am, still alive and kicking, just back in time for our family reunion, eh?"

He laughed again, leisurely feeling his battered face with his palms, letting the whole face become clouded by a hazy sense of humour. "Good joke, isn't it?"

"It is," said Sheila, uneasily. "I—I wish I could understand that joke," she then let out a short, uncertain laugh. She suddenly turned towards me as if to catch my reactions. I was smoking one of Just Call Me Joe's cigarettes with indifference. She laughed again – at the floor. I too laughed—at nothing. She let her face twist into contempt, sensing that again I was observing her.

"Would you like some coffee, my sister?" asked J.C.M. Joe, after taking his time about the idea as if enjoying the situation Sheila and I were creating.

"Well," said Sheila, looking up to him, "if everyone else is having a cup I would not mind..."

"Certainly. I'll go and boil the urn. Make yourself at home, sister."

"Thank you, my brother. Your are kind."

J.C.M. Joe went to the Common Room of the dormitory but rushed back a few minutes later to put some coffee and sugar into the cups which he had 'borrowed' from the Mess.

"Blast," he said. "We've run out of milk. I'm running up to the canteen to get some. I'll be back."

"Oh, can you get some biscuits too?" asked Sheila, searching the heart-shaped, red pockets of her checked tan dress. "*Aiei,* my brother," she exclaimed. "I have not brought the money."

"It's okay – I'll get them," said J.C.M. Joe. "Do you want anything else?" Sheila shook her head. "Brother?" I shook my head too. He left.

Sheila rose from the chair and walked a complete circle in the room, eyeing every comer of it in a way a *dim dim* housewife marks a new home. Later she said, "This room feels strange. It does not feel like last time we came in."

"I know," I said.

"It feels empty."

"It does."

"Even with those strange curtains."

"Yes."

"They are too... exotic."

"They are."

"I did not see them last time. Did you buy them?"

"Sophie got them for J.C.M. Joe."

"Oh, Sophie. She has left the University now. She has been deported for smoking Murray-Jonah—was it Murray-Jonah or who was it? I did not hear the news properly."

"Mary Juana," I said.

Strange world, I reflected, relating Sheila's idea of strangeness with mine to see if there were any similarities. The similarities were scarce, I noticed; with Sheila's, people were there, strange, but there enough to talk with; with mine the strangeness was dumb, within people that merged with time rather than appeared prominent with it, always appearing and disappearing within time, like Sophie, like Enita, like Mary, like me, like me and Mary, like me and Mary and Enita, like me and Mary and Enita and Sophie, like lonely red buoys on a rough sea.

Of course, I mused further, Sheila's strange to me and I am strange to her; but that's simple, because, come to think of it, would they really matter to each other? Really? And I was shocked by this simple thought. Frankly, I thought I had liked Sophie and the others.

Critically examining my side of the room, Sheila cried, "Why —where are your things? Don't you have any clothes?"

"No," I answered.

"*Ia madi*, this is ridiculous, my own *lalokau*, living... so poor."

It isn't poverty, I thought, what you see, sister, is my absence from tomorrow onwards."

Then to her I said, "It all adds up to one thing and one only about myself: I." I was wondering if she knew what I meant by that. I was also thinking of Sophie; no, not of the white daughter of the soil—her absence.

Sheila probably decided not to ask further about the room. Nor talk of Sophie. She walked over to J.C.M. Joe's desk and studied the typing he had done. She didn't show any interest in whatever he had typed. That's what was wrong with us; if a Papuan wrote something down on paper the other Papuans never bothered to read it. 'We already are educated without having been educated,' I once heard an Anuki student remark at the University Club. Sheila withdrew, came and sat beside me on the bed and placed her arms stiffly between her thighs. She was studying the floor like a little child.

"What are you thinking, Sheila?"

She turned. We stared at each other. Then slowly, slowly closing her eyes, as if 'hypnotised' by some strange power that was present in the room, she pulled my face towards her's.

"I am thinking about that night we came into this room," she spoke quietly.

"And?"

"And I am wondering why you said good-bye to me then."

"Did I really say good-bye, Sheila?"

She pulled her face away, opened her eyes and looked deep into mine.

"How could it not be good-bye if it was?"

"Would you want it to be good-bye?"

"No—from deep inside my heart—you know that." She stopped, bit a lip with bitterness then said, "Yet that was the only time I felt so close to you." A pause followed. "Tell me, where do you keep yourself these days? You seem so far, far away."

"I am."

"And happy that way?"

"No."

"You need me then."

"It wouldn't mean any difference."

"Oh, you do not even trust me."

Then Just Call Me Joe arrived from the canteen. We had coffee with some biscuits after which, with a cheerful yet mischievious smile, he left the room to Sheila and me. I thought of the night Sheila and I were alone in this same room. Sheila remained still, thinking. I stood up, took a cigarette from J.C.M. Joe's desk, lit it, then moved to the door.

"I'll walk you back to your dorm," I said.

Sheila nodded then lazily walked forward to meet my hand with both her's. She had barely touched my right hand when she stopped, gazing at it. My hand to her had suddenly turned into an alien colour, deformed, and was certainly not similar to her's. Then she let her gaze gradually rise from my hand to my hips, stomach, chest, chin, lips, nose, eyes—her gaze remained transfixed there. Abrupt twists of her features turned her face into perplexing expressions. She was afraid, I noticed; again, she was a very, very small child.

Instead of asking "Where are you from?" she then softly, deliberately, said, "I want to know."

"What?" I returned, and my question meant; 'I'm from a place where you have never been before.'

"First it was Joseph's battered face," she went on. "And now, your swollen hand. You two had a fight."

I nodded, thinking, "Don't get too close to my world, kid."

"Why?"

"Why do you want to know?"

"Because I am your friend. I have a right to, don't I?"

"No, Sheila," I shook my head, simultaneously employing a smile of uncertainty, distrust.

"Why not?"

"You don't know me enough," I said simply.   *

"I don't know you enough? But you are my only boy friend."

Her eyes jumped repeatedly from my right eye to my left, while her lips parted to let her tongue wet the mouth which quivered with callow scorn and confusion. "You must care to tell me. I want to know—I need to know."

"You insist, Sheila."

"Oh, but you must, you must let me."

"Then who would you blame if you knew?"

She now moved closer to me, unconscious of the fact that she had knocked off the cigarette from my fingers, and placed her arms around my neck, resting them heavily on each of my shoulders, "I will blame no one, except me."

"Not even me?" and I added, "for your sake, at least," when thinking of the possibility of having to essentially defend her in future.

"No; unless you are part of me."

"Do you trust yourself then?"

"If my conscience permits—"

"I am asking you: do you trust yourself?"

"All right, if that's the way you view things – yes. I am myself now. I trust myself." She paused, tore away from me to let out squeaks of uncertainty then, turning to face me, begged, "So please, let me know."

I closed my eyes tight: saw a dream, *a dream of nostalgic birthly eggs with changing seasons from a strange ricochet that split the yolk through weird gusts of hot metallic blood martyring spears for nude endurance in a dying universe.*

When I opened my eyes again, Sheila was waiting; anxiously.

WANPIS

He lay flat on his stomach, legs spread, arms outstretched, teeth clenched, chin tightly pressed onto the concrete pavement, ready to bloat in Moresby's thick humidity. A pair of dead eyes stared ahead of him, each socket displaying suffering, discontent, but more of established anger than anything else. His face resembled a snap-shot of a dead hero whose photographer had striven in vain to make the corpse smile again. The body was butchered by broken bottles on this hot, drunken Saturday; a gash in his bloody mess of hair, several cuts on each forearm, and a slit lower lip forming a second mouth. Constant exudations of red soaked his clothes: a dead frog in a pool of human blood. Far ahead and rapidly moving away from him were the drunken shouts, groans, clatters of broken beer bottles, flaps of flat feet, heavy metallic and wooden thuds – a running mass of humanity. War cries. *Ol lusman* on the stampede. Tribal confusion plaguing the city. The distant crowd of *lusman* yelled, jeered, cried under the blazing sun, each voice constituting the sun's heat and flames which burnt Moresby into a charcoal of national unity; an accident along the road to independence. In a moment all noise melted into a spiral of hot tropical dust, evaporating his soul in its furnace of spinning emptiness. Those drunken labourers and *lusman* had crushed him under their feet, left him to die there in the street, insignificant, without a lifetime achievement, without a history. A police van arrived at the scene, long after the fatal stampede of the drunken mass. Three policemen quickly jumped out of the van but walked indifferently round the dead frog, constantly stopping in their tracks to pick up small pieces of broken bottles and discard them into the nearest City Council rubbish bin. A few passersby stopped at the scene, studied the corpse, then nervously disappeared. More came, the curious ones, and crowded the corpse. "Is he at last dead?" an old man asked. A youngster fainted at the sight of blood. The old man, a visitor to the city, nodded mysterioulsly. A siren from an ambulance whined faintly in the distance; then it grew louder and continuous. Seconds later it appeared from the other end of the road, tore up it in its usual emergency speed and stopped near the crowd which moved, under the direction of the three policemen, to form a path for the corpse to be carried in. The red lights from the police van and the ambulance were struggling in vain to compete with the sun's glare. And already human blood was being fried and baked on the concrete pavement. After some urgent exchanges of remarks between the ambulance crew and the curious crowd, the body was wrapped in a blue cloth, lifted and, as it was being carried into the van, its eyes suddenly came to life, struggled to keep up with vigilance on the world, but immediately surrendered to a dizzy stare of reluctant helplessness. Among the curious crowd was a newlywed, young couple which studied the corpse with the same air of indifference as the three policemen. The wife, however, remarked: *"Si, mi les long dis'ela kain pasin ia.Ol wantok, yumi mas lukluk gut insait long yumi yet."* No one heard her. She frowned. Her husband, stealing a more bitter glance at the corpse, exclaimed, "Why, it's James. James St. Nativeson." The couple, caught by this sudden surprise of realisation, rushed forward as if to tear open the doors of the ambulance for a surer observation; the driver had long before turned the gear levers and the siren was whining echoingly down the road to the General Hospital. "Carelessness," thought the husband, "sheer stupidity". But upon reflection he mused, "No one else but James St. Nativeson, that All Saints' graduate, who could never afford a University degree nor any similar academic qualification but shape and mould his own talents and creativity whilst shut in a room among piles of Western Existentialist novels and essays; whilst having spent all his youth wasting away in the narrow confinement of bureaucratic clerkship; and whilst dreaming only but never becoming the country's poet and hero, its historical figure, its forerunner of free thought and honesty in the self, would choose to die like this; a battered face, squandered youth; artistic insight squashed under the weight of human underdevelopment, deaf national harmony and political dreams of pot-bellied independence." The little wife looked at her marriage comrade who had averted his eyes in time to hide these silent thoughts. "That's his problem," she decided. "He dreams too much." Then placing an arm on the other's shoulder, she said, "Husband, do not worry. We shall go and see him now." He looked at her, "I think he's had it." Then quite unexpectedly he laughed. "I've got to bless this day, Sheila," he kept on laughing; "it enabled me to see a real dead frog on the road." It was a mad rush: two young people fleeing the world of carefree thought and free exchanges of smiles and hellos, light hugs and kisses, and into the heart of sorrow, self-alienation, pretence, dishonesty and exile. They imagined Jimi Damebo was already in the Casualty Ward, unable to smile at the nurses and heave a sigh of contentment. All sensuality vanished, let alone suffering and vague expectations of a silent death ahead. "It's true about what my husband says," thought Sheila Jivi La. "One never knows when one is to die. One even dies before birth. Others, like James, have nothing better to do than decide not to participate in anything national; to just stop living." Sheila had regarded herself as blunt with thought, but that did not prevent her from being stubborn and talkative enough to be actively involved in the politics of human rights. Four years ago she had 'saved' her husband from abandoning University studies and the possibilities of suicide in a bureaucratic enclosure; her stubbornness and 'big mouth' had in fact enabled him to consolidate his pride of her and to 'regain social conformity'. And now James, who was too busy thinking of himself as a writer, forgot his own safety. The problems of change: only a few survive. One point to Darwin. "But James can't be blamed," she reasoned simply. "At least he was complete; without a University degree, without a higher salary. A home-made intellectual." They walked the rest of the Racecourse Road down to Boroko, crossed the Hubert Murray Highway, walked down along it, and halted at the bus stop. No buses came. Half an hour passed. Again, no buses. She fished out a fresh sheet of Kleenex and wiped the sweat from her brows. Then she thrusted it back into her heart-shaped pocket. Which made her conscious of the little swelling around her abdomen. She looked up at him. Before 'next fortnight' she would remind him she needed two or three *meri* blouses. One hour: still no buses. Probably the drivers were scared stiff. Her husband began to seriously sweat. She laughed softly. He swerved, alarmed. The smile faded from her face. One hour fifteen; one and half hours; no buses. A few cars hissed past, all in a hurry to get to safety. Mostly Australian drivers. "The honest ones," thought the husband. "No, not the official dishonest ones who had been localized through their own carelessness. Serve them right. One point to Darwin – cancelled. Two hours. An old bus, which was travelling through the hospital, turned up, but took a long time in getting the couple on board. It was empty inside. Sheila shouted at the driver to move on. The driver waved a hand, without looking back. Again it was a mad rush; for two. The receptionist at the Casualty Ward was absent. Probably out on a cool evening stroll at three o'clock on a hot Saturday afternoon, thought the husband. The air was silent, but boiling with humidity. He wondered if James was already in the mortuary, being frozen like fresh meat, in the Western tradition. In the village, people bury their dead quickly. The receptionist, a fairly young Australian, came rushing out from the interior fifteen minutes later, looking red and thoroughly terrified. It took her a few minutes to settle down at her desk, but she was trembling vigorously. She was unaware of the couple's presence. Instantly she reached for her white handbag, fished out a packet of Kool, a lighter, pulled out a cigarette from the pack with her teeth and lit it under a 'No Smoking' sign. The couple exchanged glances. Now here's a big girl who doesn't know how to look after herself, thought Sheila's husband. He shut his eyes with pity. A moment later, a large local nurse waded out, spoke softly to the receptionist who abruptly rose from her chair, said 'Thank you, Grace' five times and walked out. The local nurse swam the air after the receptionist to give her the white handbag which she had forgotten. 'Thank you,' said the receptionist for the sixth time; 'Thank you, Grace.' She disappeared. Pleasantly turning to the couple the large local nurse said, "Yes? Can I help you two?" "What's wrong with your receptionist?" asked Sheila. "She had a shock," explained the nurse; "she never seen blood before. It's only temporary shock. So doctors asked me to send her home and sleep it off." "Thought you hospital people were used to seeing blood," said Sheila. "Oh yes," agreed the nurse; "but not our little girl here. She never worked in hospitals before. She only came up from Melbourne three weeks ago, couldn't find a job anywhere, so she end up here. You know how it is these days. But anyway, maybe she will cope with things later on." The nurse paused and eyed Sheila's husband. "You?" she said. "Now where did I see you before? You appeared in—in the *Post Courier*, that's right. Last year?" "Last year, Sister," he said, showing no interest in the subject. "You people fought hard for our country's Self-Government and Independence," complimented the nurse. "That's my husband," said Sheila, proudly holding him by the arm. He did not smile. He asked the nurse if she had seen a fatally wounded body being carried in, "say some one or two hours ago." She had. "That the one our receptionist was frightened about." "Can he be identified?" he asked. "I mean, can your top boys know who he is?" "Just a moment, please, said the nurse, and struggled past the door to the interior. A moment later she re-appeared with an Indian doctor. The couple discovered that he was a quietly spoken, sincere human being, and felt at ease. The doctor told them the name of the wounded man then asked if they were the relatives. "Oh yes," lied Sheila, thinking, "can't let him get away with quietly concealing everything". "He's my brother," she added. Her husband winced, but decided against further distraction. "Have we any hope?" he asked the doctor instead. "One should never lose hope," replied the doctor, "even if what one's hoping for is just hope." He then explained that Jimi Damebo or James St. Nativeson was in a 'critical condition, suffering from serious head injuries'. He suggested the couple come back at half-past five the following evening and added that they should ring constantly before that time to find out about the 'progress' James was making. They gave the doctor their phone number, following the doctor's request, and left. "Think we should let Joseph know?" "J.C.M. Joe won't be interested," was all her husband said. Outside the sun still glared. A gust of wind swept up a huge twirl of dust in the air; the cloud of dust danced like a flame. "Husband," came the weak voice of Sheila; "I'm fainting." He wound an arm around her to support her. They walked to the shade of a tree and sat down. The dust ceased dancing in the air. She laughed. "It's terrible getting pregnant like this. High time you men got pregnant for a change." He said nothing. Immediately before him a ten month-old baby was crawling. It struggled to its feet, walked, wal—fell back on its back. Blood gushed from its little head. "Let's go home," he said, rising to his feet. He pulled up Sheila and they walked to the bus stop. A taxi pulled up in time to drop a few visitors to the hospital. "Gerehu?" asked Sheila's husband. The driver nodded and the couple entered the vehicle. Sheila leaned against her husband and sighed. The taxi sped on along the deserted roads. No one was sighted in this part of the city. The people were scared, too scared to move around freely even at broad daylight. They were afraid of independence. Already some of them were asking silent questions about it or him or her with fright and uncertainty. Who is this man called independence? Or underpants? Is it a man or woman or dog or what? Where is this mythical character coming from? What is to become of us all? *"Ol man pait, ah?"* asked the taxi driver suddenly. *"Ia,"* returned Sheila; *"Ol i spak na klostu kilim wanpela barata b'long mipela." "Long wanem hap? Raskos Rot?" "Ia,"* replied Sheila. *"Ating mi lukim em,"* said the driver. "Yes, *mipela nau tasol i go painim em long hospitol." "Ah. Tasol yutupela mas stap isi; no ken wokabaut tumas."* "True, true," confirmed Sheila. At Waigani there were signs of life. Few women could be seen about, however, and hence Sheila remained in the taxi while her husband went to the Supermarket for their dinner. Barely had he reached the door of the Supermarket when he came flying back to the taxi; which was unusual for Sheila to note since she had never before seen him run a few metres. "What's up?" she asked. It took him a good one minute to regain his breath after which he said, "Darling, I love you more than you can imagine, can I get us some beer please, please, please?" "Good to see you smile anyway," said Sheila, inspecting her purse; "here, get five dollars' worth." ."Five dollars?—you mean five kina." Then he exclaimed, "Five dollars?" "Five dollars it is, and get some cigarettes too." "Ah, you drink and smoke too much, Sheila. I only wanted your permission." He frowned and walked off. *"Maski, laip bilong wan wan,"* she said. The driver laughed.

"And besides, who spoilt me?" she called after him. He waved without turning and entered the Supermarket. Above, the clouds fled the sky, leaving it blue. The sun still burnt. Below a young woman listened to a story from a taxi driver of a little daughter doing her best to go to high school and later to the University, to become one of the new breed. "Times have changed from ease and comfort to hardship and suffering. Our's is hardship and suffering." (Self-neglect, thought Sheila.) "Their's is fortune and happiness." Sheila's husband emerged from the Supermarket, carrying a carton of greens, beer and other food for the body. Two seventeen or eighteen year-old mixed race girls in tight fitting hot pants followed him, licking their ice cream. "Hi," they greeted him. He turned. Yes, they were talking to him. "Oh. Hi," he said, and struggled to smile. "Coming to the party tonight?" asked the girls. "Which party is this?" "You know, Bob's. Didn't you get our invitation card last week? We've sent them to you all. We are sure we did not miss any sad one of us out. But anyway, come, just come. Jake, Sonny and Sue will be there. The whole gang will be there." "Oh," said Sheila's husband." "We'll see you there then," concluded the girls. "Yeah, okay. See you." They walked down the shops, stopping every now and then for window shopping or general peeping. Sheila's husband shook his head and blinked a couple of times out of confusion. In the taxi Sheila asked, "Who were those boyfriends, I mean, girlfriends of yours?" There was a glint of jealousy in her eyes; she quickly had her face averted. He wanted to laugh aloud, but knowing that would turn out sour dismissed the idea. "Well, frankly," he then said, "I've never seen them before. The poor kids must have thought I was one of them." She turned and looked at him full on the face. With a smile. "I'm telling the truth, Sheila." She saw pain his eyes and believed him. *"Yumi go nau, ah?"* the driver asked cheerfully. They nodded and he drove them on. The road ahead of them was clear, free. The wind whistled past them. The couple took a quick, nostalgic glance at the silent campus of the University; no souls around. They leaned back, enjoying the ride. In front of their Middle covenant Government House the metre in the taxi registered two kina twenty-six. He gave the driver the 'five dollars', leaving

Sheila to collect the change and carry the beer. Sheila brought out four bottles of beer and offered them to the driver. "These are for your wife," she teased; "not for you. Now, if you don't give these to her, you look out." The taxi driver laughed, and apparently found it difficult to promise Sheila a return favour. "Go on," she said with a laugh; *"yu wari long skul fi bilong liklik meri bilong yu tasol. Em bai winim univesiti digri, no ken wari."* The driver searched for suitable words to say but abandoned the idea of communication. He only memorised the faces of the young couple, gently nodded three or four times then drove off. Sheila ran up the stairs of their house to rescue her husband who was attempting to insert the key with his teeth while both of his hands were nursing the carton of foodstuff. "It would be easier if you placed the carton on the floor and..." She did the job herself. They entered. The interior was modest; a kitchen with a stove and fridge; three bedrooms; a bathroom with toilet; and a telephone had been installed out in the living room. The couple couldn't ask for more. Only once did they have an argument on where the rubbish bin should be placed. Sheila suggested the back verandah. He argued against the suggestion since that was the only part of the house with promises of dusk for him each day. Of course each verandah offered an optional street view that led to the other parts of the suburb. In the end the couple agreed to destining the rubbish bin under the house where the fourlegged night prowlers knocked it over almost every night. Sheila got herself busy in the kitchen while her husband had his shower. Their walking exercise of the day, from Gerehu to Boroko, has done them good, he thought; especially her. She needed that exercise, he told her, every Saturday or Sunday for four miles and slowly so that you don't sweat and wear yourself out   seeing that for three months now she had been carving an internal and serene protection for one more *husman* to the world.

see dei bin busy hurryuping
lovemaking to moni moni
and nobodies was left for to
go on living LIVE

aha ehe he i gat wok tasol
nogat time to funny funny

Flowers. These white people must be mad. Flowers indeed.
Nathaniel Tabonaboni was attempting to understand 'what is it
that makes these white people pick flowers, hold them up to their
noses, then smile possessively for a long time?' Drunk with
rapture. What is rapture? Ecstasy? These white people must be
mad. Mad: probably because he couldn't understand their anguish
and pleasures. His only understanding of smelling flowers was
that everybody else around him did. Except Nathaniel. Everyone
has been smelling flowers since the days of Chaucer. Except
Nathaniel. Even Queen Emma of the Pacific did; even Queen
Elizabeth did; even the Blessed Virgin, Joseph of Nazareth and
even the Prime Minister of Australia, did. Except Nathaniel. It
was the same as his attempt to understand those who wrote thick
volumes of books, who spoke endlessly even though there was no
one to listen to them. He was curious. Simply because everyone
was doing this—except Nathaniel. He himself loved playing his
guitar every day, composing his own lyrics derived from Jimi
Damebo's poetry; he had enjoyed listening to the recent hits of
Western popular music; he went to the cinema, went to Church, to
the local displays of random entertainment, everything else. Only
he was suddenly curious about these. Because these were 'same
as what everybody else does'. One day he'd decided to read the
dictionary out of some curiousity which he had forgotten
immediately after he had picked up the volume. He had chucked
it into the fire. Simply because the dictionary was like everyone
else. Obsolete. And this in turn had caused him to explore further
his own condition, especially in the public service. Anything he
rejected he was more than curious to know; best still he would like
to know in order to become 'objective' about them, or what he had
often termed as 'having the privilege to offer constructive criticism
on whatever you learn'. If he accepted things as they were, he told
himself, he would be what St Nativeson called 'a *lusman* without
principles'. Through James, Nathaniel had read quite a number of

books ranging from comics to the Western existentialists such as Camus, Sartre, Jaspers, Kierkegaard, even Heidegger and Ionesco. Only as little as to feel he was better off. One morning he had sat in his clerical office and laughed at his 'these white people' boss for a long time, especially after having skimmed through 'The Bald Prima Donna'. When the boss asked what the joke was, Nathaniel repeated the joke his boss told him and the other clerks the day before. The boss too laughed for a long time. So through 'heavy' reading Nathaniel had changed a lot in disposition, compared to his days at All Saints'. At the old school Nathaniel had never known loneliness: here, while imprisoned in the secluded enclosures of bureaucratic clerkship, he understood loneliness, lived it and, especially after having read a little of Camus, he could endure this sentiment of loneliness and alienation. Yet after reading one or two of Sartre's novels he became forever unsure of himself; at times he would neglect punctuality out of some loyalty he could not define. "Quite frankly, the Frenchman's just paining himself writing of me; I am the reality of his unintended intentions," James had once remarked of Sartre. "And I pity Ionesco; they're both old men now," he had added. Nathaniel remembered this day, among many others, very well when James had made these remarks. He silently recorded each word and mood of James as the poet spoke of the Western Existentialists; each mood of James offered for Nathaniel a moment for future memories, memories based on strange personal as well as spiritual discoveries. The mood he had liked most in James was that of desolation; for on this very day, James had sadly concluded of Sartre and Ionesco, "Yet we owe these old men a lot. Our debt to them is not to lose hope, nor let them down by just dying." So out of this experience Nathaniel too wanted to 'try luck' on creative writing, like James St. Nativeson. But he was 'true to himself' by refusing to do so, constantly warning himself with the thought of "Abstain, my *wantok*. The game is just starting." Which meant that he couldn't quite think for himself; he even had no idea of what exactly he had once been. And that in turn startled him to the decision of standing on his two feet against all odds, together with James, with Vera and that quiet Anuki who had preferred to stay anonymous. Only the world, he felt, underestimated him, trod on him; and for the time being he had accepted this mockery with bitter pleasure. Flower smelling indeed. *Ewa!* He spat at the pink bougainvilleas and frangipanis which grew along the top road from town to the Sir Hubert Murray Stadium. Just for fun he walked over to the paradisical garden and picked off a white frangipani; he held it to his nose, smelt it, sneered at it, then began tearing it to bits, petal by petal. A dog barked when he neared one of 'these white people's' residences. He stopped, so that the dog would change its mind about biting him. The dog rushed at him along the edge of flowers, jumped over the fence then onto the road where he stood, frozen. It barked once, twice, thrice. Dogs that bark don't bite. It bit him on the shin. Shocked, Nathaniel darted for the nearest frangipani tree. The dog followed and was now barking directly beneath him. Should it not be browsing away on a hot day like this? An Australian stood at the door of the residence, tightly holding a pink baby in her arms. Nathaniel expected her to shriek orders at the dog to retreat. 'Stop it, doggie. Stop that barking at once. The poor boy's only enjoying his stroll.' Nathaniel tried to transmit the words into the lady; his lips were quivering soundlessly. The woman just watched the scene with her baby for one, two, three, four, five seconds, then disappeared into the house. 'There are natives around,' Nathaniel assumed this to be what she thought. 'Must be rapists. Such people don't need help'. The dog kept on barking. Two policemen in uniform strolled past, sweating, smoking cigarettes and exchanging dirty jokes in dialect. The dog was desperate to have another nab at Nathaniel. He broke a branch of the frangipani tree, made a club out of it by stripping off its leaves and flowers then hit the dog hard at the ribs. The dog interrupted its own barking with a short yelp and fled. Nathaniel grinned bitterly. His teeth flashed from his sweaty and polished brown face. His wound from the bite was now exuding dark, red blobd. The blood of his disposition, his innocence, his soul. Flowers. He swore and spat again. So he was right after all. They still mocked him. He resumed his hot Saturday afternoon walk. He sweated profusely. He felt the loneliness churn within the deep waters of his own bitter loneliness. He shouldn't have walked this stupid road but for James St. Nativeson who had decided, for the first time during their friendship, not to tell him where he was going that morning. Probably out watching drunks, hot Saturday town village idiots and city rascals in all forms of dress and manners, just to return and write a paragraph or two of his novel. Yes, Jimi Damebo had abandoned poetry and was now working on a novel—'to startle the Third Black World'. So the first places Nathaniel had checked were the two public bars in town. He had walked into the crowded Top Pub; no sign of James. He had tried the Bottom Pub; still no sign of James. He had wanted then to catch a bus to Boroko, to check at the Calypso Bar but abandoned the idea simply because he had no money. Kone Tavern, which was the shortest and easiest to go to, would not be an interesting spot for a writer. And Palm Tavern was just as dangerous. So he had ultimately decided to take the afternoon stroll back to Newtown Hostel, using the top road along the side of the hill which overlooked Moresby Harbour, Konedobu, Hanuabada and Baruni. The deep blue sea rose to meet his eye with rich, silvery stars reflected by the hot tropical sun. "No, it's no use.. It's too hot to marvel at the bloody sea. No more, no more native traditions of seaside romanticism." He thought of Vera, of James, and stubbornly dismissed the recollection that he did read "The Plague" once, "The Outsider" twice. "Oh, come on, let's not repeat a sad history." But memories of Vera and James still lingered. Vera, Nathaniel was now consoling himself with his own defeat, had read more books than Nathaniel, possibly more than James St. Nativeson. She didn't, however, talk much. But she was amiable enough at times, and had shared everything freely with James and Nathaniel. One Good Friday afternoon, when St. Nativeson fled the horrifying silence of Newtown Hostel to the University to see Just Call Me Joe and his Anuki companion, Vera visited the native clerks' residence in search of Jimi Damebo. She found Nathaniel in James' room instead and casually asked, "He's not here." "You mean James?" returned Nathaniel and asked himself if Vera had asked the question or said it. "Yes," answered Vera. He said, "Sorry, he's gone off to Uni. to see Just Call Me Joe and Anonymous. " "Who the hell are they?" asked Vera. "Oh, friends," shrugged Nathaniel, "as much as James, as much as Nathaniel, as much as Anonymous, as much as—as …you?" Vera entered the room. Sat on James' bed. Then pretending to remember, she rose suddenly and extended her hand. "I am sorry," she said, "my name is Vera—James' friend or a friend of James." "I've heard of you a lot through James," said Nathaniel, accepting the other's hand; "a pleasure meeting in person, Vera." She sat down again. "You are James' room-mate." "No, Vera," smiled Nathaniel; "just a friend. My room's in the other block. I just come up here to do some reading. Anyway, my name is Nathaniel or Nathy for short. Friends just call me frogface." He laughed. She didn't. "So James' room-mate must be on leave," asked Vera. "Oh yes; you are quite right." That was all Vera seemed to want to know or talk about. She had never met James St. Nativeson's room-mate since she began visiting the Local Clerks' Hostel; which also meant that the room-mate was absent. An intellectual absence. On James' desk were some exercise books, note pads and manila folders. One of the thick exercise books was casually titled 'Random Notes for the Novel'. She picked up the book and opened it to the first page. Notes. Nothing but random notes and plans for a thick volume by an amateur writer from an underdeveloped nation. From that page Vera mentally read, 'The characters in this novel are not just literary inventions; they are based on the friends I currently treasure, and without whose personal sacrifice in terms of intellectual contributions to the content of this book, I would never have attempted an effort as ambitious as this. Where necessary the reader should not fear the liberty of assuming that anyone of these characters can be an autobiographical representation. I am indebted to... 'Vera turned the pages; she wasn't interested in the 'I am indebted' bit nor was she in the mood for careful reading—no, not when she had come all the way from Boroko just to discover the absence of Jimi Damebo. And Jimi Damebo was always missing, whenever there was an appointment for him to meet with any visitor. An interested editor of an Australian literary magazine might come looking for him, simply because James had a tentative poem or short story published in a literary journal somewhere which has some relevence to the literature from the underdeveloped nations; he may ask at the University from where he will receive no hint of Damebo's whereabouts; he may enquire at the Department where James works and still he will learn nothing. This is the writer's terrible fate, thought Vera; in reality Jimi Damebo does not exist. From the middle of 'Random Notes' a passage drew Vera's attention: 'Even now, while planning this novel, while treating it as a spare-time hobby, I am afraid. Afraid because I am too inexperienced to attempt an effort as ambitious as this; as such I feel I am fooling over two and a half million people. Above all, I am afraid because I and I alone, and not one or two of the so-called creative writers in this country, asks this question'. What question? But Vera was so much bored by that incommunicable Good Friday afternoon she did not bother reading further to find out. She let the pages of the hand-written literature fly until she stopped at the last page of 'Random Notes': 'This is the first and last dawn which I am too stubborn to embrace. And what a choice! I can't even have a good, tearful laugh about my sad destiny; nor beg the world for recognition. Yet at the same while my life is full of coqtradictions based on adolescent and studentship convivialities, yearnings; today I run, tomorrow I expect forgiveness for my foolishness. The case is the same with this dawn: there are no definitive enough forces to help create that self-determination in me; every book I read is simply a dream which automatically gets crushed by the next book I pick up. I am all confusion. Why should I be frightened of saying this? And my condition is as poor as the society which constitutes me; one moment I adore loneliness; the next, this loneliness is tormenting. But what more have I to add to that—this loneliness is tormenting? I am not a fat priest in solitary confinement to masturbate, nor a married Christian to vie for another's wife. My senses are dormant, dead. My eyes are blurred not of ageing but of self-neglect and pride within these dead dreams of becoming a famed idealist. Almost anyone can agree that, right now, I torment myself being alive. The others are just simply blinded by this dawn, and thereafter have only the dreams of a potbellied future and beer-stained independence to resort to. All I have left are self-dejection and complaints which enable them to remark:

"Ah, but we should not release our problems upon the world. Rather we should strive our best to save it". With me I have to read Camus to ensure that, an experience of insight quite beyond their comprehension. To them there is no difference'. After that page was the title of the novel. Vera opened it to the first chapter with anticipation. Nothing. Just white paper. She looked up at Nathaniel who had his head buried in a small volume about the size of a cigarette packet. The volume was 'The New Testament'. "Shit," thought Vera, "'the poor bugger must be lonely." She then asked, "How well do you know Jimi Damebo?" Nathaniel looked up from the Bible with a smile; "We went to the same school." "All Saints"?" "Yes." "A pity," said Vera; "we had been just ninety miles from each other for four years and we never met." Nathaniel smiled again, meaning he knew very well Vera went to Soya Pier High School. "And after that," he then asked, "Where did you go?" "Keravat Senior; but I had abandoned the last year, simply because I needed money." "'The same with us all," returned Nathaniel, without emotion. "Have you any girlfriends?" Vera asked suddenly; she had expected him to be embarrassed by the question. He wasn't. "'To be honest, I'm a *lusman* without principles," he said. "I don't appeal to girls much." "So you don't have any," Vera clarified the other's answer. "No." "You know what you want, but you don't try hard enough." "That's true, my sister. I am too timid. Either that or I don't understand girls." This boy needs help, thought Vera. "'How close are you to James as a friend, Nathy?" "Very close, without the sexual aspect of the phrase." He was staring sternly at her with the remark. "To be exact," Nathaniel went on, "I stick to Jimi Damebo because I admire the kind of man he is. And, well, he's a friend I can't afford to lose. Without him, as I said, I'm the *lusman* without principles." "I think I like James for very much the same reasons," Vera said, trying to socialise; "apart, of course, from the fact that he and I grew up together." Then she added, "Which is just childhood fantasy." Nathaniel looked down at the Bible again and remembered it was Good Friday. 'Peter said to him, *"Even if all turn away from You, I will never!" Jesus told him, "Truly I tell you, during this very night, before the rooster crows twice, you will disown Me*

three times. " *But he asserted more insistently, "Even if I must die
with You, never will I disown You.* " And so they all said.' Nathaniel
shuddered. He looked up to find Vera gazing down at him, her two
hands resting on each of his shoulders. "Come," she told Nathaniel;
"let's make love." Nathaniel was shocked. No, this is not possible.
It won't, it won't, it will never happen. It never does.' He stared
with pained incredulity at Vera. Vera stared piercingly back at
him. She meant what she had said. He stared straight ahead at the
shelf where James stored the books. "You are worried about
James," she asked. "Well..." began Nathaniel but – "It's all 'right,"
confirmed Vera Nonda'isiri; "he will understand." Rising
awkwardly, Nathaniel rested two uneasy arms on Vera's shoulders
and said, "Sister, I need your word of honesty." There was silence.
Then Nathy stammered, "I mean, I—I don't want to betray James
St. Nativeson." "Everything that is mine is yours as much as
James St. Nativeson's," said Vera. Nathaniel attempted a smile
which only caused his cheeks to quiver with guilt. When Vera held
him closer to her flesh he felt comfort and peace. For the first time
in his career as a clerk Nathaniel felt that he was born again. And
Vera knew that there were no greater sacrifices as significant as
this. "No, no, no; I won't accept it, dear. It's like begging for it."
An internal peace escaped Nathaniel's flesh. He stubbed his toes
on the bitumen and his thongs went flying to the other side of the
road. The voice of a woman came from a house, just above him,
on the side of the hill. The woman, another Australian, was
scolding her child for possibly a certain mischief or request which
Nathaniel had missed. "No, dear," she was repeating, "no." The
child, around seven or eight by Nathaniel's judgement, just stood
stiff on the green lawn, hands by his side, gazing contemptuously
at the woman who was standing on the steps and, stamping a foot,
whined, "Oh, Mum." Nathaniel picked up his thongs and hurried
barefoot down the slope to the Sir Hubert Murray Stadium and up
to the hostels. In his room he put a wild pop record on, full blast,
and lay on his back on the bed, trying not to dream but think. It
was an unsuccessful attempt and his eyes wandered around the
room at random. The music was blaring away with distortions and
without Nathaniel's shame. Posters of sorts, mainly blow-ups of

pop stars ranging from Elvis to Jesus Christ Superstar, hung carelessly all along the walls. Nothing about the room was tidy. Last year, he remembered, his room-mate had hung himself in this same room. The situation was similar: the room-mate was an unhappy clerk who returned to the room after a brief Saturday morning walk, stripped, turned the same record player full blast, then took his own life.

> In that mirror wherein my hero
> had numerous visions of quiet and numbed
> tranquility ....youthful
> in a Mekeo hairdo: so tall, so sensuous;
> dangling animatedly at the end of a thick
> rope that came down from the ceiling.

The rope still hung in the room, only shorter since the ambulance crew cut it to remove the dead body. No one knew where the dead clerk came from although Nathaniel had guessed, judging by the room-mate's constant cursings in a familiar dialect, that he was either from the Raba Raba Sub-Province or Northern Province. Nathaniel jumped down from the bed and, on tip toes, attempted reaching the rope. *"Tambu,"* a voice called without knocking on Nathaniel's door. *"Ewa,"* he called back; "that's the third time I been startled today." He angrily opened the door and a New Ireland youth stepped in, striving his hardest to let his short and slim body tower Nathaniel by placing each hand at his hips. Nathaniel furiously jumped onto his bed and remarked, "When you have reached that height, kid, I'll let you know." He then jumped down again and imitated the New Ireland youth; they were both the same size. "Bloody cockroach," Nathaniel then muttered and turned away; "bloody gingerised cuscus. What's wrong with some of you Tolais and New Irelanders—being born half-cooked by dusk like that?" He switched the record player off. "Well, what is it?" he asked the youth. "Phone call for you," said the youth, disregarding Nathaniel's anger; "in the Warden's house." *"Giaman,"* glared Nathaniel. *"E;* true, *tambu,"* said the New Irelander; "I just came over from there. There's a girl on the phone, probably er, you know." "Bullshit." *"Ei,* tomorrow's

Sunday, *tam bu. Mi no giamanim yu."* "OK, I'll run over now. But if this is one of your stupid tricks again, you look out." "I won't look out because I'm telling the truth," said the youth and entered the room to play Nathaniel's guitar. The Warden of the hostels was a friend of Nathaniel's; or a busy clerk who personally knew every resident there. "Come in," said the Warden; "there's a girl on the phone." "Thanks." He picked up the receiver. "Hullo, Nathaniel speaking." "Oh hullo, my wantok," came the voice of a female; "thought we've lost you." "Sheila," he shouted at the receiver; "I know you – you nut. How are you?" "Not too good." "Oh? Drunk again?" "No, you idiot – worse." "You are pissed then." He could feel the soft giggles at the other end of the phone, and his flesh vibrated with yearning. "How's your man?" he asked. "He's still anonymous," came the voice of Sheila; "Now you just shut up and listen to your old mother, Nathaniel..." She told him about Jimi Damebo. Nathaniel shrugged uneasily. A cloud of dismay passed over the sunlit virgin jungle of his soul. Black footprints stained the azure of his visions, his future dreams. Nathaniel just stared at the empty air before him, mouth agape. He then relaxed and through the mouthpiece said, "Thanks, my *wantok. Amapo ananae anainanai."* "We've been there," came the voice of Sheila in a tone of insistence; "The doctor said we can't visit him until five tomorrow evening, when they might have some good news for us." Tomorrow's Sunday, thought Nathaniel. It was going to be a nice holiday. To the receiver he said, "How Vera must be hurt. Have you told her?" "No, we've decided not to rush things, for her, at least." "That's good, Sheila. It's well that you haven't." He paused, scratched an ear and then said, "I'm only wondering how I can tell her the news." "I have a better idea," offered Sheila; "now you just relax, stay calm—" "I will, Sheila—" "—and go to her hostel now—" "—I can't now, Sheila." "Why not?" "I have to prepare myself for the Fellowship; er, you understand—I mean, I must, I must—" "Well, please yourself, Nathaniel. But are you going or not?" "I will, Sheila." "All right, then. When?" "Half past six, this evening." "Okay. Good. Now, tell her, when you go, that I have invited her to a party—" "At your house?" "—Yes. Just tell her that. Nothing else. And for goodness sake, appear lively."

"Trust me, Sheila." "What about your Fellowship?" "I'll take her to the Fellowship. She may not like it, but I hope she keeps up. The Fellowship finishes at 9:30. So would you still let us in as late as that?" "Sure. Come any time you wish. But be here..." "We will." "Good. I'll just ring her up now and let her know you are coming to pick per up." "What if she asks about James?" "Tell her James is missing; he doesn't exist." "I 'can't do that," exclaimed Nathaniel. "I know you can't. But knowing Vera, she does have a good sense of humour." Nathaniel laughed. Which wasn't funny. Click! Something went wrong, thought Nathaniel. This isn't James. He doesn't move around much, especially with his weak lungs. Jimi Damebo had been coughing excessively since he had starts cigafette smoking at All Saints'. Upon three occasions during his career as a clerk, Nathaniel recollected, James had coughed vigorously and exuded dark, red blood from his lungs. Once Nathaniel had seen him lie in bed for three weeks and thought the end was near. It was then that Jimi Damebo, between tears and through a weak laugh, stammered, "Brother, I know this is crazy, but I—I feel like going back to Church." "I'll take you to Church," Nathaniel then offered, and the following Sunday, when they had finally gone to Mass, James was healed after receiving Holy Communion. It was a miracle, according to Nathaniel, which James doubted. Now it seemed that the ultimate end for James had arrived. "Bad news?" asked the Warden. Nathaniel came away from the phone. "Yes. Er, you know how it is with girls," he lied. The Warden indicated with a nod that he understood, then added, "You can't trust women." He was not married. Nathanielleft him in a hurry. In his room the New Ireland youth looked up with a grin. "The Lord be praised," he said, "I'll be your best man at the altar." "Ah, sharrap," snapped Nathaniel and, grabbing a bath soap and his towel, left for the shower blocks. He returned a few minutes later, threw the towel and his clothes on the bed - "Hey, you are not stripping in front of me, are you?" - got into his fresh jeans and Tshirt, combed his hair, wore his white runners then, to the youth, said, "Get the hell out of here. And leave my guitar alone. The last time you borrowed it there were three strings missing." The New Irelander raised a hand in protest. "Look, I don't care what you do," said Nathaniel; "you leave, you sit here and play that guitar or do anything, but there isn't going to be any practice this afternoon." "Oh?" said the youth and strummed a few chords; "So we just appear in front of the others and pretend we are Simon and Garfunkel, eh?" "It's you who needs practice," retorted Nathaniel; "you'd better get your A and B and E minors organised. The last time we played you just sounded like a frog freshly recruited from a village string band or something." The youth remained calm. He admitted within himself that Samarai boys like Nathaniel were natural guitar players and musicians. Slowly he rose with the guitar, walked over to the desk and pulled out Nathaniel's music notes and song book. He opened the song book to a selected page and started playing and mumbling, "E, A minor, G, B, minor, hold, one, two, three and a half – F/A minor/D..." "Hmm," said Nathaniel and walked out, slamming the door. He strolled down the street, hands in his pockets, walked around the Sir Hubert Murray Stadium and finally reached the sea wall. He thought of going to Vera then, but the sun was too low. Later, when the pick up bus comes by, he decided. Besides, in such times of trouble a man's got to be alone with his thoughts. He felt serenity and absolution in him, but his heart sank. The sea was his sorrow; sprinkles rushed at him, thrown by the high tide. These formed tears in his eyes. He wouldn't see Jimi Damebo till Sunday. And Jimi Damebo was already dying; an alien death; in a foreign soil. The sun was dying out on Nathaniel, on Jimi Damebo, on the world. In a moment it would hide itself behind the hills at the other side of the harbor. Nathaniel got onto his knees and prayed for forgiveness; then he asked Jesus to save St. Nativeson. He forgot about the bitterness he had against "these white people". He forgot about flowers. The pain in his wound from the dog bite was gone. And he felt new. Like a wayward wanderer who accepts Jesus for the first time in his life. He returned to the hostel and found the New Ireland youth with his guitar. He apologized for getting cross. The youth just asked him to listen while he played their song right through. They walked down to the Mess, had dinner, then returned. In his room they both played their song again and Nathaniel said nothing. Their bus turned up at six o'clock and they boarded. Friends from the Fellowship were in the bus, all with smiles, singing happy spirituals to the rhythm of their guitars, ukuleles and other instruments. Nathaniel asked the leader of the Fellowship if they could go to Boroko and pick up 'a friend who is interested in joining the group'. The leader agreed and they drove on to Boroko. Vera was waiting for Nathaniel in her room. Their meeting was happily brief for Vera. But upon seeing the bus, she said, "We are not going in that, are we?" "It'll only be three hours, Vera. And anyway, I thought you'd like to hear a new song we've derived from James' poetry." "I don't mind," said Vera, minding. Nathaniel introduced her to the group. The leader shook Vera's lifeless hand and said, "Welcome to the Fellowship, sister. Hope in time you might like to join us." "I might," said Vera and forgot to smile. The hall was packed with young Christians, most of whom were University students together with those who had abandoned their original Churches. Among them was Nathaniel's and the New Irelander's music tutor, a tall Australian in silver-rimmed spectacles, and always making sure her dress covered her knee caps. A young Christian once remarked that if whe was as anxious as all that, it was high time she bought a new dress that covered her knees without much bother. She walked over to Nathaniel and said, "So? What's the song we are hearing from you tonight?" "At the break of a Dawn", said Nathaniel. "Oh, that's right. We wrote the music of it last month. Now, let me see. James… James…" "James St Nativeson wrote it as a poem; then Peter and I wrote the lyrics." "And have you invited James this evening?" "Unfortunately, I couln't catch up with him. He's always busy, you know. And – oh yes, this is Vera. James' friend. Vera, Miss Stork, our music tutor." "How do you do, Vera – Jennifer Stork." The two shook hands. The leader asked for everyone's attention and after a few announcements the group settled down to evening prayers. Vera obediently joined the group, but every time Nathaniel caught her eye she employed stares of discomfort. Once she stared at the ceiling without tilting her head back for a long time and Nathaniel squeezed her arm. "I'll kill you after this," she whispered. "Cool it, baby, cool it," whispered back Nathaniel. The prayers which included group participation in songs with guitars, ukuleles and other instruments came to an end. All helped themselves to chairs at random places and the leader resumed his authority. "Brothers, sisters and friends in Christ," he began, "tonight as you are aware we are continuing with our individual and group performances of original music and songs. Tonight, of course, we hear the last of the performances and then the judges should let us know of the winners, which should be on Monday, at the latest. But first let me thank you all for coming." The leader paused, walked over to a girl sitting in the front row, had a silent conference with her, then returned to his original position. With a smile he said, "Our Secretary informs us that the bar is open." There was applause and clapping. Under the din Natahniel leaned over to Vera and said, "We only drink Coke and things." "I believe you," said Vera, anxious to leave as soon as possible. "Now," said the leader, "can I ask you to walk over to the bar and get your refreshments? And please hurry, because we have to get our performances well under way." The young Christians rose and walked over to a section of the hall where the Secretary served them with drinks. Nathaniel said, "Can I get us anything?" "I'm saving my emptiness for the beer at Sheila's." "I think I'll do just that," said Nathaniel. "Excuse me, Vera," he then said and walked over to his New Ireland friend for last minute advice. He returned. Said nothing. The leader announced that the first of the last performances was about to start. All seated themselves comfortably, silently sipping their lolly water. Someone coughed. It was the leader. "We will open up the show with the New Ireland Choir. They are our brothers and sisters from the University. Reminding you once again that our judges are Miss Stork, Brother Jacob Nangojoe and Mr Kenneth Tovero. They are up in the fron row. So we start. Brothers and sister, The New Ireland Choir." All clapped except Vera. The choir, composed of four boys and two girls, walked up to the front and sang three chorals. Two more groups followed and then it was Nathaniel's and his friend's turn. The pair walked up, both with guitars, and took their places in front of the one microphone for the hall. Nathaniel cleared his throat. "One Way, brothers," a girl called out to the pair and they both bowed with gratitude. "One Way Jesus."

Nathaniel cleared his throat again and there was silence. "Brothers
and sisters, friends of Christ," Nathaniel spoke and Vera sensed
that something had gone amiss. Stage fright? No, not with
Nathaniel, she decided. "Our song tonight is not a happy one,"
went on Nathaniel. "It has been written by a fellow who isn't a
Christian any more but a grat friend of ours – that is, me and Peter
here – and the song itself has in it the deepest of spiritual emotion
and experience." Vera noticed that Nathaniel appeared tense but a
little contrite, employing every now and then his usual bitter grin
as he spoke. She waited. "The song involves all of us, I believe;
what we feel when we wake each morning, our hopes, our fears,
our losses and the more darker side of our lives. But in it, I was
glad to note when I first read the song in its poetry form, there is
hope still." He paused. A new girl to the Fellowship, sitting next
to Vera, leaned over to her girlfriend and asked, "What's that
boy's name?" "I mean," continued Nathaniel, "almost all of us
have seen that film in which 'Amazing Grace' was ung, and we
felt the kind of suffering Christians go through. But let me make
a plea, brothers and sisters, that although the composer of our
song isn't a Christain he should, at least, be understood along the
lines that his songs and poetry reflect the people we are. His name
is James St Nativeson, originally Jimi Damebo, but he had
changed his name, probably because he is a *lusman* like everyone
of us." The group stirred. A few giggled. "Now with us here
tonight is Vera, a friend of James and before Peter and I sing the
song could you give her a cordial welcome, please." The young
Christians turned to Vera, clapping, and Vera put on a blind smile.
"I have known James St Nativeson for over seven years,"
continued Nathaniel. "During that time I've learnt a lot of things
from him. I've learnt, for instance, that loneliness is desiring
others to know you exist. But loneliness can also be retained in its
most human significance. I've learnt tolerance, patience and the
art of enduring all forms of suffering from James. Above all,
James had enabled me to recognize my condition, to understand
my destiny, and to stand on my two feet as a Christian and face the
world with its trials and betrayal, its falsehood and truth. I have
thus come to the conclusion that people like James, like Vera here,

like Anonymous, had experienced deep human suffering. Yes, with Christ Jesus we get to know these people and understand that their suffering is ours also. And although suffering is immense, and if one is a Christian, there is hope still in the air that surrounds one." "One Way, brothers. One Way Jesus," called out the girls. Someone whistled. "Our song, brothers and sisters," concluded Nathaniel, "is 'At the Break of a Dawn' by James St Nativeson." Immediately the pair attacked the guitars, concentrating on the minors chords until the melody flowed out, the words of the song conspicuously audible, and filled the hall.

At the break of a dawn
A certain kind of song
Broke into my heart and second thought
Giving me those strange illusions about her
Knowing the things you've done
Still aren't the same as anyone would

When will we learn to see to reason?
All we embrace now
Is to have that old
Birthright to the sing the most
Common songs upong this earth.

The group remained motionless, as Nathaniel and his friend carried the room away with them, in search of dawn, in search of laughter, of flowers and sunlight.

Ravidi maisene
ku paika kurigu
bi mataririm'ma yam nuavisi
ku veregu na a nogota wosim de.
A kovi da kudu .
boga i rabaraba Ououooh.

When at last the entire poem of the song became what everyone thought it meant, a glass of claret broke in Vera's heart. She shuddered; her fingers felt a new warmth which she could not define. A strange kind of sensation swept through her soul.

And in her youthful days
dreamt of her in some strangest ways;
yet was I caught in a pool of pain
and from a rootless dream I thought of her
all the world came to be
one great big chain of my reprieve.

Miss Jennifer Stork saw a country inhabited by sunlight, olive trees and brown grass, and dead artists crudely displayed along bitumen streets, bloating in the heat.

So when this cloud of curse
will have to come to pass;
and when my scissorsed mind will have to be healed;
fresh green trees will grow along Waigani Road
I shall then rise to shine
with the well-wishers of my time.

Kapore nuguguru kam tubuga
kitana warae
kam bodu iyi
muri bi wawayim kuyi
nago waiwaratete.

"One Way," shrieked the girls in the hall. "One Way Jesus. One Way, brothers." The gathering cheered, clapped and stamped the floor with their suede shoes and barefeet. By now Vera was convinced that something had indeed gone wrong. She noticed that at times during the song Nathaniel prolonged certain words, let them hang on the thread of his shaky voice with the help of the microphone and the audience's concentration and the stilled night air, and with his eyes shut, as he let his soul slowly, deliberately crawl out, until the floor of the hall vibrated beneath him, under the weight of his discontent. When Nathaniel came down and joined Vera, she said nothing. The Fellowship bus drove them to Gerehu. Sheila met them at the door and led them in. There was no party, and Vera's heart sank. They all stood in a ring, silent. Sheila got Nathaniel's guitar, disappeared into a room, then re-appeared without it. She said nothing. Vera broke the silence; "I suppose you people are going to tell me that James St Nativeson is missing, that he doesn't exist." Sheila's husband cleared his throat, then said, "I'm sorry, Vera. He – " "He's in the hospital," said Vera. "How did you know?" exclaimed Nathaniel and threw a frightened glance at Sheila. "I felt it. All women do." Seating herself down on the visitors' bed in the living room, she said, "Get me a a beer please, someone." Then suddenly she shot up from the bed and banged her face against the white wall, simultaneously hitting the I white wall with her fists and sobbing vigorously. "Oh James. James." She swerved, glared and shrieked at Sheila's husband. "You cheats, you bastards, you bourgeois pigs. Why didn't you tell me when you rang this afternoon?" Sheila's husband shut his eyes, but remained frozen. "We've feared the worst – " offered Sheila. "Feared the worst my foot. Do you realise what you have just done? Hah? You've taken me for cheap, for a village idiot. Christ, Sheila, I'm no child." She broke down to sobs again, rushed for the telephone, but stopped, lifted her head, shut her eyes, turned and faced the others. A short shrug broke her body loose and she sank onto the floor, defeated. Sheila and Nathaniel helped her to her feet and led her to the bed. "I'm sorry, I'm sorry," she then said. She relaxed, camly lit a cigarette and extended her hand to Sheila's husband; "Beer, please." He brought out a bottle, opened it and gave it to her. She quickly gulped half of it. "And for Christ's sake, look alive. We are having a party, aren't we?" Sheila and Nathaniel joined her. Uncertainly. "How much beer have we?" she asked a little later. "We've got a carton you've asked us to get this afternoon," answered Sheila. Vera opened her purse and brought out a note. "Here's your money then." "Keep it," said Sheila. "Thanks," said Vera, but crumpled the note, walked over to Sheila's husband and thrust it into his shirt pocket. "Double-faced, carbon—copied, bourgeois pigs," she said and drained her bottle. "And the worst ones at that," she added; "some village idiots pretending to be all supreme and powerful without any knowledge at all of the bourgeois means and philosophies of existence. Christ." She placed the empty bottle on the sink, opened the fridge, brought out another, and walked back to Sheila and Nathaniel. She opened the bottle with her teeth, but took her time with the beer. "When I say we are having a party, I mean it," she said, in response to which Nathaniel danced to his feet and, half-singing 'don't get me wrong, don't get me wrong', walked over to the record player and put on Jesus Christ Superstar. The others felt comfortable. Sheila's husband asked Nathaniel over to the kitchen and said, "Brother, there's beer here, a bottle of bacardi and some dry wine. They are all yours." "Thanks. Let's concentrate on the bacardi while the girls drink beer or wine, shall we?" "Now hold on, fellas," shouted Sheila. "We have to eat something first. "Yeah, let's enjoy the party," agreed Vera. They were all smiles.

James wondered if he could live again. He did not care what happened to him, and even if it was a question of life and death, he felt he had done enough living already. Still, his senses responded to the morning sounds of another day the same way everyone else's would and he tried to sit up. He felt numerous chords force him back to the bed again. He opened his eyes wide. Blank. They had bandaged his whole head up. None can see through darkness. Only James St. Nativeson. Who tries. He struggled to see light. Saw darkness. His flesh and insides ached. 'Jesus bloody Christ. What's happening?' A female voice comforted him by his side. '"Listen, sister, whoever you are..." The nurse cut him short: "Don't speak. You'll only make your wounds worse." He resumed endurance and silent suffering. He was Jimi Damebo again. The whole room of his ward, he could now imagine, was filled with silence and James St. Nativeson. Outside, the familiar morning sounds grew louder. He felt at ease. And waited. Waited.

Anonymous Anuki woke up before the sun. His head ached. He was not used to waking up early, especially on Sundays. He leaned over the naked flesh of Sheila and parted the louvres and the curtains. The whole suburb was asleep. From the hills in the east, just above the slumbering suburb, came the obliterated red glow which proclaimed the arrival of the sun. He thought of that trip from Soya Pier to Posa Bay; he missed himself in the days of his youth. It was beautiful, he thought of the period; and innocent. He thought of Mary; of Yaguyawa-Kuburina; of the woman called Enita. But his feelings for them were as remote as one having little or no history attached to one's life. Sheila turned and pulled him down on her. "Careful now," he winced; "we don't want to squash the kid." "Who's pregnant, you or me?" she laughed. She then said, "It's too small yet; deep inside. Only fluid." She played with him, "Come on, let's make love." "It's already daybreak." "Coward." She won. And dropped off to sleep again. On top of him. He carefully moved her over to one side of the bed and sat up. It was still dark in the room. He jumped out, stumbled into the bathroom, urinated, then returned. From his room he noticed that the lights in the living room were on. He went into the bedroom, quickly got dressed, then came out again. Vera gave him a careless wave of her band and with a dull smile, she said, "Hi." "Hi. You didn't sleep." "No; Nathy and I went and got another carton soon after you two retired." "I see." He saw Nathaniel sprawled on the floor, sound asleep on his stomach. "Have a beer," offered Vera; "or are you still the bourgeois pig?" "Might as well," he said, "to get rid of the headache." He went for the fridge. It was full with brown and green bottles. A *lusman* bar, he thought amusedly and pulled out a bottle for himself. Joining Vera, he said, "Dawn's here." She said nothing. Her bottle was empty. He went and brought her another. They drank and smoked without talking. Every now and then he looked out of the window to watch the progress of the new day. The sun rose over the hills, a red and orange ball of yolk, falling onto a frying pan of brown earth; he remembered James St Nativeson and wondered if the poet was awake.

> It is 6:30 a.m. on Sunday:
> on the louvres where dead curtains fall
> fattened mosquitoes perch, unconfessing of twelve
> hours' blood sucked out of me as I lie still,
> away from Morning Prayers and Holy Communion,
> complaining of growing old at twenty-three.
> *Aia, na dubo-vevera ena.*

He looked at Vera. She remained calm, studying his eyes. Drunk? Vera just stared: wonder if he's as good as James in bed. Nathaniel stirred, turned over on his back, and groaned. He opened his eyes and saw them. He laughed, jumped to his feet, but fell onto the visitors' bed, drunk. *"Ewa,"* he exclaimed. He struggled to his feet, again staggered to the *lusman* bar, tore open the fridge and brought out a bottle. The bottle was too heavy for him and he fell with it to the floor, laughing noiselessly. Vera and Anonymous just watched him from the living room. "Think... you'l kee'me pinn'd down 'ere... ay?" Nathaniel asked the bottle while opening it with his teeth. He drained it. After which he stolidly rose to his feet, a different man. He robot-walked to the record player, planted his feet firmly there, but noting his own clumsiness turned to Sheila's husband. "Put 'im on... will yer?" "Who?" asked Anonymous, and he felt his own voice sound more Papuan than Nathaniel. "Tha' stupid record... or anybody... anybody 't'all... so's we can 'ave music. Right? Yarright-hic." "Oh," said Anonymous and walked over to the record player, but afraid the music would wake Sheila up, withdrew. Vera got up from her chair, confidently, proceeded on a normal walk but lost courage half-way to the door of the bathroom. Her body slid down the wall. All sensitivity, no longer captivated. She laughed aloud, then swore in dialect.

> On my door to Room 13
> only the wind sighs past,
> indifferent, no longer alive.
> It bloods
> tears of welcome to those stranded in the streets
> with whom I share conversations ancestral
> 'tween black twist fumes and crimson spittles
> of a nation's conscience-massage betel nuts.
> *Aia, 0 Aia, na mando i tae, i tae.*

Anonymous switched the light off and looked out of the window. Crimson light flooded the living room. He opened the door to the front verandah. Sunlight soaked his body. Lit up his face. A dull tan. The dull tan made him conscious of himself, as a man, a resemblance, even an imitation of that idea of absence. He

winced. Then, alarmed, he turned suddenly to Nathaniel who was
too drunk to notice him. He relaxed. He would wait for them to
drop off to sleep. Then he would ring the hospital. He went out to
breathe in the fresh morning breeze; 'inhale deeply through your
nose, keep the air in for five seconds, then breathe out through
your mouth; repeat this till the sixth time.'

On the floor where the sun streaks in
SP bottles rest in careless drunken slumber
among last night's pisspasted vomits
flies wake to buzz at quarter to seven
against a lone voice from the radio
which claims it ain't scared O' dyin'
while I greet the infernal rising sun
refusing promotions in the Public Service.
Aia, I have lost patience;
O *Aia naka,* I have lost all endurance...

Fourth, fifth, sixth time; his lungs felt fresh. He re-entered the
living room and decided he needed a cigarette. In the bathroom
he heard Vera pull the chain. She staggered out a while after
that and sank into her chair. "Well!" she said, but forgot to add
anything else to that. Anonymous switched on the radio and again
a lone voice declared it was not scared of dying and that 'when
I'm dead and gone, there'll be one more child born in this world
to carry on'... "Who the hell are they?" Vera asked of the singer
on the radio, and Anonymous turned the volume up. "'Blood,
Sweat and Tears', I think," he said. "Are we alive and kicking?"
Sheila came flying out in a floral nightgown, quickly kissed her
husband, Nathaniel then after Vera, added, "Or dead?" "Hey, hey,
hey," Nathaniel swayed like a coconut tree to his feet. "Come
'ere, woman," he beckoned Sheila in a drunken hoarse voice.
"You people chicken'd out, hah? But don' gemme wrong, don'
gemme wrong, baby; we jus' wan' some 'elp wi'tha' beer. Right?
It's more impor'an' fiss' finshin' - ah fucken - finishing tit than
gettin' drunk, right? Blurp. Right." "Sounds as if you two stayed
up all night." "Ah, 'ave a drink, Sheila," said Nathaniel. "Gonna
chicken out again, are yer? *Ewa.*" He dropped back on his chair.

The usual smile of bitterness swept across his face. "Well," said
Sheila, clapping her little palms, "what you need is breakfast and
some sleep." "Save the paternalism for your welfare job, Sheila,"
said Vera; "I'm getting drunk."

Since his appointment to his new job in the public service Just
Call Me Joe had resumed his Christian and traditional names. He
preferred Mr Joseph Bikman to Just Call Me Joe. He was quite
successful in his career; so much so, in fact, that luck escaped
his grip and for the time being he was content with just being a
bachelor. He had asked eleven girls for marriage, most of them
nationals and including Sheila Jivi La. They had turned him down
with excuses such as 'I am concerned with my studies' or 'job' or
'am engaged to be married next year'. The Australian or European
girlfriends that he used to have had either been deported or had
simply decided to return to their own countries. All he had left
were letters from the 'chicks' he had known during his study tour
overseas. In the village he would easily have a wife, Nathaniel once
remarked sadly. Mr Joseph Bikman deliberately forgot his village,
his parents and relatives even though they were still in existence. He
was 'in fact, a heterosexual homosexual,' Vera had once described
him in an off-handed way; 'always in the company of males and
preaching endlessly against homosexuals.' That Sunday morning
the telephone at his flat rang. Who could be ringing at seven
o'clock on Sunday morning? Christ, not Father Jefferson by some
ill chance? He got out of his wet bed. Or Archiebald Goldsworth?
It's about time that *lapun* was localised; unless the old warrior was
anxious to get himself a PNG citizenship. He walked over to the
low table of his living room where the telephone was installed.
"Hullo, Mister Joseph Bikman speaking." "Hullo, Mr Bikman," a
high-pitched, female voice answered, almost on a mirthful verge
of mimicking Mr Bikman, and he had to hold the receiver at a
safer distance from his ear. Then meekly, with his eyes rolling like
tennis balls on water, Mr Bikman said, "Hullo, who's speaking,
please?" "Sheila Jivi La," came the pleasant voice; "remember
me?" "Yes, of course, of course, how are you?" "I'm okay; how
are you?" He told her he was fine; that he had been very busy in

the last few days; "you know, all these executive meetings and
constitutional meetings and law reform meetings and ombudsman
committee meetings and so on and so forth." "Oh. Thought I'd
ring you up about James. Thought you'd be interested to know."
"Which James is this?" "You know, James St Nativeson, the
poet." "Oh. Oh. You mean Mr Jimi Damebo?" "Yes, if you'd like
to put it that way. Anyway, he had an accident yesterday – I mean,
a crowd, probably drunkards, rushed and attacked him and he's
in the hospital now." "Oh. That's sad. That's sad." There was a
pause. Mr Bikman was anxious to get back to bed. "Well—well
what do you want me to do about it, Sheila?" "Oh no, nothing. I
just thought I'd let you know. Like all his other friends." "Well,
that's very kind of you, Sheila. Listen, I'll just write out a che—"
There was a sudden click and Mister Joseph Bikman shrugged his
huge body helplessly, his eyes dancing like ping-pong balls.

"Parauma," said Sheila; *"Parauma natui."* She glared at the
telephone then turned away. "Who was it?" asked Anonymous.
"Your old friend Just Call Me Joe alias Mister Joseph Social
Derelictus Bikman." Sheila was furious; she kick viciously at the
empty air and paced the floor with rapid steps. *"Ae,* this kind *ia.*
They won't go to heaven. If I were in charge of the gates of hell
I'd kick him straight into the fire. One day. One of these days I'm
gonna have a good woman to man yarn with Just Call Me Joe."
She was still pacing the floor at the same pace. "What did he
say?" asked Anonymous. Sheila stopped pacing. She turned. She
tore open each socket of her eyes, peered into her husband's face
and, mimicking Mr Bikman, said, "Ooh. Ooh. That's sad. That's
sad. But what do you want me to do about it?" "Let me get at
him," shouted Nathaniel and rushed at the telephone. His drunken
personality had suddenly disappeared. It was anger. A *lusman's*
rage. Sheila pulled him back: "You are not going to help build up
my telephone bills, are you? Besides, you know what they'll do
to you if they catch you swearing over the telephone? You'll be
finished. *Kalabused.* Now, you just sit down, relax, and enjoy your
beer." Sitting down again, Nathaniel calmly said, "'Bloody fucken

hul pekpek-sucker bastard." He jumped up again, but walked naturally to the *lusman* bar for refuelling. Vera was preventing herself from dozing off. She rose, staggered to the radio, switched it off, found a Simon and Garfunkel record on the shelf, put it on, then said, "'Nathy and I will take care of your electricity bill this fortnight, Sheila." Anonymous went to the telephone. No one took notice of him until he yelled, jumped up and down twice, then heaved the longest sigh of his life. The others swarmed around him. Covering the mouthpiece, he said, "He lives." "The Lord be praised," shouted Nathaniel and drained his bottle. Sheila was muttering a prayer of thanksgiving. Sunlight flooded happiness into the living room. A dove left the earth and fluttered in the clear blue sky of Vera's soul. "So? We are visiting him this afternoon? Asked Sheila. "Just a moment," said Anonymous and asked the same question into the receiver. Silence, except for the song from Simon and Garfunkel, returned to the room. Anonymous' face turned calm, retaining its usual composure. "Thank you, " he said and gently replaced the receiver. "Well?" asked Sheila. "There is hope still," he said, not sounding hopeful. "Don't lie," said Vera. "Well, he's alive. That's the main thing." "What did they say? What did they say?" insisted Natahniel. "They said there were some complications the doctors had to iron out first." He turned to Vera. "They also wondered if they could have our permission to—" "Let no newsman or broadcast intruder come near my man," interrupted Vera. "'Where were they last year and the years before?" She fumbled for the packet of cigarettes she saw on the floor, retrieved it, but found it empty. She threw the empty packet at Nathaniel. "Go get us some cigarettes." Anonymous leaned down to her and said, gently, "He is still alive." She looked up at him fully and said, "Who said he is going to die?" Nathaniel left for the cigarettes. Anonymous followed. The women were left alone. The streets of this new suburb came to life with people. Under the warm morning sun there were pleasant smiles and free exchanges of remarks; 'certainly devoid of Western mentality', James had once described the blind mood of happiness in the faces of these people. Another Town Sunday. "Do you go to Church these days?" Anonymous asked. "Not often," answered

Nathaniel; "the Fellowship is all I have left, though, but more than I can ask for." "What do you call yourself then?" "A free believer of Jesus – without the bureaucratic *giamanabaut.*" He laughed. "And you?" Nathaniel asked. "Sheila does. Sometimes." "What about you?" "I listen to those wonderful composers of the world, like you and James." Flowers danced in the sun; children scurried and giggled all around them. Anonymous threw his eyes down the main road of the suburb, at the colourful sight of Town Sunday goers, all talking, smiling, laughing and waiting for buses. Each bus that turned up at this section of the suburb was already full.

Town Sunday:
strangers coming
people going
souls meeting
merging
melting
clean and common
in a happy unity
of dedicated confusion.

They walked down the main road with the crowd, turned right to leave the Sunday goers, then walked further into the interior of the low cost housing area where they found the suburb's only trade store. They had to push their way in since the trade store was crowded. A woman complained that someone had touched her bottom. "Whoever the man is," she spoke aloud in Motu, "I hope he goes and fucks his own mother." "You are the mother," someone in the pack remarked. A young girl screamed in the middle of the pack, but wriggled her way out to the open, giggling. "The holy brothers are at it again," said Nathaniel; "every Sunday anywhere in Moresby I witness this same happening." They bought the cigarettes and left the crowd. On their way back they saw a bus pull up near the Sunday crowd. The crowd rushed at the vehicle, some of it attempting to get in through the windows. Those from inside the bus pushed the desperate ones back onto the dust, screaming, "No room, no room." "Then why stop?" asked the frustrated ones from outside. "Ask the driver." The driver finished lighting his cigarette, turned the gear lever and the bus squeaked its way onwards, along the road to the University, to the city. Only a select few deserve a ride to heaven. Those that were left behind still looked their Sunday best. "Wonder what they do in Church nowadays?" thought Anonymous. "Probably get themselves legally registered for the World-After." A few girls, who looked as though they were bored with waiting for the buses, walked past them. One smiled at Anonymous then found it difficult to take her eyes off him until she dug her shoe into the rough gravel, after which she swore and ran after the others. He ran his fingers through his hair and remembered he had not had his morning shower; then he realised that he had forgotten to remember Sheila Jivi La, immediately after which he was remembering to remember her. "What's reminiscence?" he asked himself. "A memory; a personal reference, like 'home'?" In turning the query over in his mind he forgot Sheila which made him remember her. A tricky business being married in the Church, he concluded. "Think he's really had it this time?" asked Nathaniel. "Who?" "Jimi Damebo." Somewhere in the shaded parts of his conscience, Anonymous felt a crack, a skull broken, and slowly, inevitably, poisonous black blood began leaking into the brain. "I don't know," he said.

> Today I cry:
> 'Life is taken
> and I resent
> I must reject
> premeditated spiritual
> assistance'.

The blood leaked in, choking the cells. "There are some complications the doctors have to iron out first."

> Why, there is magic in the air
> and spells are cast;
> predetermined witchcraft,
> anxiously revealing
> wombs of a society.

"What are you hiding from us?" Anonymous imagined Vera asking him. They left the Sunday crowd once more and walked back to the house. Sheila was in the kitchen, labouring away for breakfast, pausing every now and then to exchange brief conversations with Vera who just sat on her chair and drank. Vera was observing Anonymous soon after the men had arrived from the trade store. He felt uncomfortable. He wanted to say, "It's not my fault, old girl," but dismissed the thought. Nathaniel opened a packet and offered Vera a cigarette. She resumed studying Anonymous through the bluish fumes, as if waiting for the moment when Anonymous would show the first sign of fear. "Why is she picking on me?" thought Anonymous. But his face remained calm, silent. Like All Saints'. "It's terrifying having artists as friends." He smiled at Vera. "More beer?" "No, you bastard," she said; "my bottle isn't empty yet." "I know. That's why I asked you." He was grinning. Sheila announced that breakfast was ready. She suggested they all sit at the table. They all did. Unconsciously. After breakfast, all except Sheila went out to the back verandah, drinking, smoking, and watching people and cars pass by. The street was empty. Then they saw a white Honda sports car come tearing up the dusty road at careless speed, bobbing up and down on the rough gravel like a frog. Upon passing them the driver beeped a dull croak of a horn and waved to them. "Soabaness!" Anonymous yelled to the driver, with a jump to his feet. The Honda disappeared round the corner. "Thought he was a wantok of yours, husband," Sheila called. "In a way," returned Anonymous, sitting down, "in a way." "Wonder what he writes nowadays?" queried Nathaniel. "They don't," offered Vera; "they just drive around in second hand cars pretending to look posh and important." He was immediately forgotten. They forgot Town Sunday and talked literature, music, village customs and traditions; Nathaniel brought out his guitar and played some songs derived from St Nativeson's poetry. The white dove that was fluttering in Vera's blue sky now circled the earth below in tearful observation, waiting. In the living room, Sheila kept herself busy with the telephone, constantly announcing to the others that James was 'doing just fine'. Anonymous asked Nathaniel, when

he got back to the hostels, if he could collect all of Jimi Damebo's
writings and put them in a safe place, 'preferably bring them
up to the house.' "I will," said Nathaniel; "They'll be safer up
here, I think." "And with your permission," Anonymous said to
Vera, "I would like to use the material." "How can I trust you?"
said Vera; "You are no artist, nor even a *lusman* or *wanpis.*" "I
know I'm not an artist, Vera, but you artists and creative writers
must reillise you need people like us. Not Just Call Me Joes;
not even that scallywag who just drove past in his Honda; no,
not even the public service side of me and Sheila." "I'll drink to
that, husband," called Sheila from within. She was drinking cold,
weak tea. "How shall we begin," asked Vera; "and where shall
we end." "We've already begun," said Anonymous, "and we'll
never end." "I don't get you," said Vera. "Well, if you don't get
me, grab me." The others laughed. Vera swore. "You are all the
same," she sighed. "You enjoy promoting dead artists on the road.
And like the rest you just expect them to get their fat carcasses
off the ground and start walking." "There are others worse than
us, Vera," said Anonymous. His eyes appearred hurt. "It is only
anticipated that the guilt of all this is shared," he added. "All right,
have it your way, brother," said Vera. "But bear in mind that I
haven't changed my thoughts about you being a pack of fleshy
wastes of the real Western bourgeios arses. Get me a beer please,
Nathy." "I'll get it," Sheila' called. "Anyone else for more beer?"
"Two more please, Sheila," answered Nathaniel. Sheila brought
out three, opened and served them. She went downstairs with
the empty bottles and carefully stacked them in a carton. They
had to sell the cartons of empty bottles for their electricity bills.
She came up again and entered the living room. Her little wrist
watch read two minutes to eleven and she switched the radio on
for Sunday morning ring-for-a-record. "So?" asked Vera: "How
can you get your material published? They won't accept any of
Jimi's work up here, and down south they look for high quality
stuff." "Oh, I'll write to a couple people I know in Australia, all
right," said Anonymous, thinking, "Now how the hell do they go
about publishing things?" He shut his eyes and found himself in a
huge conference hall. Hundreds of people filled the hall, listening

to a Mr Abel Willborough, President of the James St Nativeson Creative Arts Fellowship. The President was emphasing the fact that the awards, which totalled three thousand kina, were granted only to those who showed potential in – Anonymous opened his eyes with a start, only to catch himself being watch by Vera. Her stare was piercingly menacing. "Think I need another beer," he laughed. "Your beer is there, right in front of you," said Vera.

Life. Fingers strived to feel their way out, to feel the warmth of the air, to feel the sun. Fingers that were deprived of sight, but still retained human sensitivity. A man was talking to the world from pitch darkness. *Wanpis*. The fingers moved, folded, stretched then travelled down each edge of the bed. They stopped. Thinking. "I am tied down. Some of these *bineis* should cut two holes for my eyes to see," J ames said aloud. His lower lip bled. White bandage soaked red blood. "Don't try to speak," the female voice at his bed urged; "It's only us." "Who's us?" "Just you and me and the world," said the nurse. "The Lord be praised," James tried to laugh but could not. "They teach you worse things, sister. You know, speak soft to the man who has only a few hours of life left, make him feel at home... ah, what could be better than lying on top of you on this bed, sister... " "Just lie back and relax," the nurse was pleading; "don't think... " " ...ah, you pack of bastards and bitches; you pack of lost sheep, *Aia Goudi.*" He stopped. Rapid whistlings could be heard from his breathing. His lungs ached. "Bet it's Sunday today," he then managed to say. "It is," said the nurse; "now don't try to talk, dear. You are bleeding." "Ah, *nanse,*" he let out a weak sigh, the sigh of defeat, then dropped back on the bed. Above him, on the ceiling, were faded brown patterns of life, human figures deformed and blended with animals. Below was the dusty wooden floor that had never been swept and polished for a long time. A gust of dry wind invaded the room through the louvres; papers flew in the air, but settled on the floor. A folder fell from the desk, fell open on the floor, and handwritten poetry flowed out of it. Jimi Damebo's heart quivered with shock; it has to be his poetry that must die.

"Husband," exclaimed Sheila from within. Anonymous rushed into the living room. She pointed to the telephone. He picked up the receiver hurriedly, but remained tense, frozen; still earth, serenity. Vera and Nathaniel entered and joined Sheila to watch him. He spoke quietly to the phone, said "That's fine" three times, placed the receiver slowly then turned. Vera's eyes caught his. "They said he has just dropped off into unconsciousness." "Oh," said the others. The white dove in the clear blue sky had vanished. "Well, let's get back to our drinks," Vera helped Sheila and her husband with their conscience. "Good idea," said Anonymous. They went out again, leaving Sheila in the room. Later she brought out more beer for them. "Twelve bottles left," she announced; "you'l have four each." "Aren't you drinking, Sheila?" "Don't be silly, Nathy. No, not in my present condition." "Oh, I'm sorry." The streets of the suburb were again empty. Most of the inhabitants were in the city, colouring it with their brightly coloured dress, hot smiles, sweaty cackles and Town Sunday giggles. Gerehu was deserted. Sunlight scorched the brownish earth. "Another desert," thought Anonymous. In a cube walled by thick concrete and mud, bright flowers withered; a thin line of fracture let the black blood leak in, killing the flowers, the poetry. Anonymous opened his eyes with a start. Vera was no longer interested in him. She was employing a far away look down the road that led away from the back of the house. "His poems will live," said Anonymous. Vera looked at him. "No," she said. "Why not?" put in Nathaniel. "Because," said Vera. She was watching the road that led away from her. The white dove was discovered amidst the brownish *kunai,* shivering and exuding blood from its beak. A taxi pulled up at their side of the house and blew the horn. "Who's it for?" asked Nathaniel. In answer to his question Sheila came flying out in her fresh clothes, ran down the stairs, across the lawn, greeted the driver – it was the same man. He gave Sheila some cooking bananas and pumpkin tops. "Oh," protested Sheila, but the driver forced her to accept the gift. She returned with the bananas and pumpkin tops, stored them in the kitchen, then ran out again. From the lawn she called, "Won't be long, wantoks. Just want to get something for lunch."

The taxi drove her away. "Let's talk of happier things," offered
Anonymous; "you don't mind, Vera." "No, no; it helps." "Hey
we've missed ring-for-records," exclaimed Nathaniel, rushed into
the room, grabbed the transistor and came out calling, "It's still
on. It's still on." He placed the transistor in their midst and they
chatted while listening to Tom Jones shouting about a daughter of
darkness. Nathaniel sang along with Tom Jones. "And what are
you doing with your sexy life from tomorrow onwards, Nathy?"
asked Anonymous. "Oh," he said, then turning a glance of guilt at
Vera, added, "got a girl in trouble. Guess I'll marry her and have
it all done with." "Your happiness is all that matters," said Vera.
He smiled, looked at his feet, and bent his head. A drop of dew fell
from his face, creating a work of art on the floor. He looked up at
the two suddenly. "Now that wasn't a happy thing to talk about,
was it?" he laughed through watery eyes. "Be a man," commanded
Vera. He dried his wet face with the back of his hand then, sniffing
through a weak laugh, emptied his bottle. He then apologised;
felt comfort. "What about your Lahara Course, Vera?" asked
Anonymous. "That was ages ago," said Vera, sounding a little
upset. "Anyway, for your info. I've passed it. Had even done first
year while you buggers were trying to set yourselves up in this
house; but abandoned the rest." "Think of going back?" "I can't,"
said Vera; "I'm not interested in university degrees, anyway. Have
applied for a fellowship down south – in literature and art, of
course." "Been writing much lately?" "I'm working on a play.
Contemplate entering it in a compo in Queensland soon." "Now
we are beginning to grope our way out, eh?" They laughed. At
themselves. And Sheila returned. She ran up the back stairs with a
brown parcel, said *"Ol wantok, yupela stap yet?"* and entered the
room. She was sweating. She went to the bathroom, had another
shower for the day, got into yet another set of fresh dress, and
came out to the kitchen again. She started labouring for lunch.
"I'm tired of this," said Vera, staggering into the living room. "I'm
tired of this." The two men entered after her. "Tired of what?"
Sheila asked, passively. "Tired of waiting." Vera sank into a chair,
but immediately jumped up and started staggering towards the

bathroom. In the mirror of the bathroom she pulled a face and spat into the sink.

> My hero woke up one morning
> to be shamed by his twenty-first birthday:
> the mirror told him he had no love
> no ancestors to look back to
> to claim he once had life.

Nathaniel was strumming his guitar and singing in an imitated, half-choked Rod Stewart voice, but his song was more a narrative than music.

> My hero was never a happy man.
> Heard a rumour he had a girl once
> down at YWCA: she died
> in an Anglican vestry long before he was born.
> People said he was mad, he should go to Laloki
> to convalesce - even his closest clerical
> acquaintance offered him half-a-beer and a fag
> (following the dinkum Aussie tradition) as a joke
> on the latter's poverty. My hero he just
> took one quick gulp, chewed the bottle
> then kindly advised the fat donor
> to tie the noose around his own neck...

Tired of strumming, or searching for the right chords, Nathaniel threw the guitar on the visitors' bed and decided upon reciting the narrative.

> My hero turned away in outspoken anger;
> he cursed; he wept perplexing tears
> that fogged his visions of internal consolation:
> and to the stubborn wind that hissed by
> he cried: 'Ah *Mama*. I have seen the *duk duk*
> tonight in commercial underwear.
> But where is the beautiful *tubuan?* only to
> hear his own echoes: *"Na tubuan we?*

Mama, Tubuan we?"

Nathaniel moved around the living room, his eyes shut, his fingers tightly gripping an imaginary microphone which he held to his mouth. He was in a large hall, filled by thousands of faces, in white shirts and Afro-Asian cloaks, and which constituted the black race of the Third World.

> In his room
> at the poverty-stricken Local Clerks' Hostel
> came the storming havoc of my hero's mania
> that could redeem a nation: Jesus Christ
> Superstar posters tore down from the walls
> in whining protest; Bibles remained shoemarked
> and the music roared wild at full-blasted distortions
> in response to the imaginary crowd in the mirror
> that cheered, jeered, boohooed, mocked and spewed
> at my hero as if he was a wounded matador (but still
> a hero) reaching in a fit of tremor-riddled ecstasy
> to grab his own life from the bull
> of social acceptance and rejection...

"Vera," exclaimed Sheila and rushed to the bathroom. She found her vomiting into the toilet. She helped her to her feet. "I'm sorry," said Vera; "shouldn't have done this." "What you need is a good sleep." Vera washed herself and Sheila led her to a bedroom. She sighed, lay back, weakly called out her mother's traditional names several times, then darkness smothered her conscience, her soul. "How is she?" the men asked, when Sheila came out. "She's sleeping." "What I need," Nathaniel counselled himself, "is a good hour's sleep. But first," he grabbed his guitar, "some music, bacardi and coke." Sheila laughed. Anonymous sat down, relaxed, then remembering, got up and walked over to the kitchen. He pulled Sheila to him, wrapped his arms around her, and kissed her on the mouth. "What's come over you?" He grinned, said nothing, pulled out the bacardi bottle, the coke, two glasses, and walked back to Nathaniel. The two men drank and sang in broad daylight. Like *lusman*.

A stiff, lifeless foot knocked the bacardi bottle over. Its remaining content spilt on the floor. The two men were drunkenly asleep. Sheila sat alone at the table. No one joined her for lunch at three o'clock that afternoon. She poured herself some cold tea and had it with two ham sandwiches. Then she tidied the interior and exterior parts of the house. She took out the bananas and pumpkin tops the taxi driver gave her and threw them into the rubbish bin under the house. She collected the empty bottles and once again stacked them in the carton. She wanted to wash the floor of the living room; but that would mean having to wake up the men first. She sighed; gave up. She went to the bedroom and returned with a note pad and a biro pen. At the table she wrote notes. Finished, she pushed her chair out, placed her feet on the floor, walked to the phone, picked up the receiver and dialled a number. Then, uncertain, she replaced the receiver and consulted the telephone directory. Satisfied, she dialled the number again. Silence. She waited. Silence. "Oh hullo," she spoke with a start into the receiver. "Hullo, boss. Sheila Jivi La here." She explained or read the notes from the pad. Waited. "Yes, I'll do that," she then said. "What about the Archiebald Goldsworth Community Welfare Fund? Think we could use some of it?" She paused; frowned. "But Felix," she then said, "there's this business about paying closer attention to those directly or indirectly attached to All Saints' High School." She listened. "Yes; he is. He is an ex-All Saints' student. Yes. That's right. Er, James St. Nativeson. Rather, he was Jimi Damebo. Yes, I think that's the name he uses for official purposes. Yes." Pause. "Yes. Okay then. What's that? Oh, he's sleeping. Ha. Ha. You don't say. All right. Ha. Ha. Yes. Okay, Felix. We'll see you tomorrow. Thanks very much." She hung up. At the table she wrote more notes, then went and put the pad and the pen away. She returned. Nothing to be done. From the shelf above the record player and the transistor, she brought down a copy of *The Cross and the Switch Blade*. Got to see the film again some time. She loved Pat Boone. Settling on the table, she began reading. Outside, the dusty streets came to life with the afternoon Town Sunday crowd. The Europeans drove through the streets, sending up continuous wisps of dust in the air. The crowd moved aside to give them way, then the pattern of the crowd returned to form a pious line in that dust. A woman was complaining aloud that it was time the streets were sealed with bitumen. Sheila left the book on the table and went out to the front verandah to find out who the woman was. It was an elderly, large woman, most likely wife of a senior public servant. She was hustling her children to keep well off the road as there were more cars passing. The cars gave them more dust and left them. The woman coughed; with each cough her fat belly jumped from her groin up to her chin and back again; her skirt bobbed up and down. She was too fat, Sheila decided, and settled down on a chair at the verandah. The wind whistled against the fly-wires of the house; the afternoon was getting windier. The crowd decreased; doors were being opened and shut in the other houses; verandahs were being occupied. The day was dying away. "Nothing to do," exclaimed Sheila. She was not in the mood for sleeping. She thought of writing a letter to Papa; or Paul at All Saints'; Mama scolded her in her last letter for not sending her some money, so she would be obliged to reply that letter. Then it occured to her that she had no brothers -, sisters - , or relatives-in-law. Wonder how it feels like to have a mother-in-law? A father-inlaw? She felt guilty; it was as if she had kidnapped a lonely soul out of nowhere for marriage. But she saved his soul, she thought. Saved him from abandoning University studies; encouraged him to keep on with his studies until graduation, after which, this house, modest but a home anyway. And in the years to come she would see his promotions; and hers; they would own a car, have two or three children, even buy off this house from the Housing Commission. She was drawing out a fair amount of fortnightly salary; like her husband she started work with over two thousand a year, so that between them they were saving about a hundred a fortnight. Felix was a nice sort, she mused; he knew his job well as a psychologist. She only wished her husband did a job as interesting, rather than be shut in a room as a simple administrative officer. Laziness and self-neglect, that's what she called it; now here is a husband, a fairly educated Papuan, who sits back on his bottom, relaxes, and expects humanity to fall from out of a clear blue sky and land on his lap; here's someone who believes that the other Papuans are as clear-sighted as he is, so that in time they will say of him, 'Listen, don't you think it's time this man deserved a name?' But she loved him, as much as Vera, Nathaniel and James, because they were *Ol lusman*. "Aren't we all," she exclaimed, and suddenly found herself pitying Just Call Me Joe. "The man's mad, lost. More so than most of us." She wondered why her husband did not show the slightest emotion towards Just Call Me Joe. "Just forget him, Sheila," he had once said simply. "But we could, at least, change his mind?" Sheila had tried to argue. "Not Just Call Me Joe. Sorry." "Wonder where they end up?" The sun was sailing away from her side of the house. Careful not to wake the men up Sheila entered the room quietly. She got the book from the table and neatly restored it to its usual place. She stood and watched the men. Nathaniel was snoring. Her husband just reclined on his chair, his head tilted, and using the white wall as his pillow. A frown swept across Sheila's face; he was already awake and staring at her through an amateur smile. "Thought you were drunk," she said, pulling him up from the chair. "Just felt sleepy, that's all." He went with her to the kitchen, wondering what he should do. "Haven't you anything better to do?" she grumbled. He shrugged sadly; "Wish I were a writer with all this spare time. Writers don't have time, you know." With that he disappeared into the bedroom, only to reappear with a foolscap pad and a biro. He sat at the table and looked out of the window, tapping his teeth with the biro. Sheila laughed at him until, exhausted, she vomited into the sink. "Pregnancy," she cried out contemptiously; "bastard." "Not at the kid, Sheila," he protested in alarm. Nathaniel stirred, sat up. His eyes appeared blood-shot, sleepy, *"Ewa."* He staggered to the bathroom. Sheila went to the cupboards that were along the corridor leading to the bath and bedrooms and pulled out a towel. Vera came out of a room and leaned against the wall, watching Sheila. "Sorry," she then said; "I slept too much." "Don't give it a thought," Sheila said; "you needed that sleep. Here, use this towel." Vera got the towel, placed it over her shoulder and walked out to join Sheila's husband. "I too fell asleep," he said apologetically. "I'll have a shower and go back to the hostel," she said. Nathaniel came out of the bathroom.

Sheila was struggling with a cupboard. He helped her pull it open, so that she could clear the way for him to return to the others. Sheila pulled out another towel among the white sheets and extended it to Nathaniel. "You need a shower," she said. "You people must be rich, having spare towels like this," complimented Nathaniel, but reluctantly re-entered the bathroom. Sheila walked out, and to her husband and Vera she said, "We must be hungry." "Why not?" the two chorused, as if hunger was just an idea. Vera offered to help Sheila in the kitchen, but the other refused the offer. "Well, at least for as long as Nathy's in the shower." "Okay then, Vera. You take charge of the chicken. I'll prepare the greens and some rice." The women set to work. Vera noticed that the bananas and pumpkin tops were missing. When she turned around to look at Sheila's husband, he was smiling at her. "What a nut," thought Vera, and brutally drove the knife into the chest of the dead chicken. "They think they'll get away with it." Sheila never bought taro and kaukau; not even fish and delicious crabs from the market. An elderly villager had once informed Vera that this sort of people devoured meat that was already decaying. Carrion eaters. Eaters of carrion. Wonder if they are Papuans, at all. She was now exemplarily butchering the chicken to pieces. Serves them right. Nathaniel came out of the bathroom, his hair well moulded into a Mekeo hairdo, and looking clean and fresh. It was his favourite joke to appear that way; at most times he had paid little attention to his overgrown fuzzy hair. He joined Anonymous at the table. "Short Story? Poem? Play?" Nathaniel asked boyishly, peering into the pad in front of Anonymous. Sheila's husband pushed the foolscap pad towards Nathaniel; it was empty—white and empty. "Oh," said Nathaniel and rose with the pad to his feet, "Oh. Oh." The women came out of the kitchen to cast stares of curiosity at the men. Nathaniel, studiously raising the pad in front of him, burst out laughing: "Verbose, verbose, verbose. *Ewa.*" "I've done my best, as a Papuan," Sheila's husband muttered helplessly. Nathaniel kept laughing. Anonymous then surprised himself with the thought that he himself was not good at laughing at his own jokes. He felt uneasy—not with Nathaniel but with the sentence he wrote. "Since when," Nathaniel asked, "did you start

writing this one word?" "Since birth." The others saw anger in the
eyes of Anonymous. He looked away. "What do you plan to do
with it?" laughed Nathaniel, displaying his usual air of 'cool it,
baby, cool it'. "Give it to the house boys at Konedobu for
publication? They love writing dirty things under your name."
"Yeah," jeered Vera from the kitchen; "they'll recommend it to the
tourist board for you." "Cheats. Liars. Thieves. Murderers." The
voices came in from outside. Nathaniel stopped and wiped the
tears of laughter from his eyes. He and Anonymous looked out of
the window, past the back verandah; they saw five or six children
playing *kung fu* on the road. The children stood in two lines,
facing each other in *kung fu* poses, growling, then yelling and
showing neat rows of white teeth. "Thieves. Liars." one line
called. "Cheats. Psycho-murderers." "That's a new game,"
remarked Nathaniel, forgetting Anonymous' creative effort.
"They've grown tired of hide-and-seek," said Anonymous, also
forgetting his own writing. The women returned to their work.
"Can you ring us a cab?" Vera asked Sheila's husband. "You are
not going now, are you?" asked Sheila. "No. After. When we have
dinner. You don't mind." "No, no," said Sheila; "you haven't
eaten since breakfast." "My turn to shout us the fares, Vera,"
called Nathaniel; he then laughed as if checking himself, "next
fortnight. Well, not that I'll be rich then, but we got to travel safe.
One death is enough for us all." Then they remembered James St.
Nativeson. Guilt in the form of silence filled the air about them.
"What's the meaning of death?" thought Anonymous. Warriors
yelled, raced to and fro, the directions of their ambush interweaving
—in his mind. Arrows flew, spears clashed against wooden
shields; clubs smashed their way into a human skull; a man was
crushed under the weight of hundreds of barefeet; his blood
spurted, reddening the green grass. The tribal warriors vanished.
A ring of curious crowd moved in on the victim; the dead man
rose to his feet, thoroughly annoyed, but solved the shattered
jigsaw puzzle of his own skull, brushed off the dirt from his own
clothes and excused his way out of the ring of bewildered faces,
muttering, "That's the third time I've been held up here."
Anonymous wanted to let out a cry of victory but dismissed the

desire, deciding it would only be foolishness; the others' foolishness. Men were born to die; James St. Nativeson couldn't exceed death; and that's what the others believed. Which was the 'unmelting reality'. He looked at Nathaniel scribbling on his foolscap pad, just below his one-worded creative effort. Nathaniel was drawing a man playing a guitar while sitting under the palm trees, at dusk or in the morning; Anonymous could not make it out, but there was a round ball just semi-circled by the horizon. It could have been in the morning. A *lakatoi* was sailing across the white semi-circle; the *lakatoi* was a silhouette. "Can't you be consistent?" said Anonymous, disappointed. "What do you mean?" Nathy said, afraid that he might have had lost his artistic talents. "That," said Anonymous, pointing to the drawing, "Is it in the morning, at dusk or midday?" "Dusk, I should say," said Nathaniel, and held up the drawing at a distance for the both of them to judge. Anonymous winced. "Oh, all right, all right," muttered Nathaniel, putting the pad on the table again; "look, for your sake, I'll just put in a few flying foxes. One there, another, and one here. There." He held out the drawing again, "satisfied now?" Rising from his chair like an art connoisseur, Anonymous said, "Your man with the guitar is romantically singing away on a hot, sweaty, tropical day at half-past six in the cool of the evening." "That's right. That's right," exclaimed Nathaniel; "let's call it Papua New Guinea art then." The women in the kitchen giggled. Anonymous ambled about the living room. He was bored with the afternoon. Nathaniel was bored also; they all were tired and bored, lazing the afternoon away. Or waiting for art and poetry to die with the coming dusk. The odour from the kitchen made Nathaniel's mouth water. "I have a word of significance to utter," he announced, joining Anonymous with the ambling; "It's going to be the philosophical statement of the day. I am hungry, like a man." "We all are hungry, like villagers," corrected Anonymous. Vera walked past the men and went to the bathroom; upon her reappearance ten minutes later Sheila announced, by consulting her tiny wrist watch, that dinner was ready. The women prepared the table and served the food. Which was an imitation of the classy Goldsworth dinners. Anonymous sat at one end of the table, leaning against the white wall and facing Sheila opposite him. On either side of the table were Vera and Nathaniel. Nathaniel said grace; Sheila joined him in the 'Amen'. Then Nathaniel felt rich protein and coconut oil sting his throat; he swallowed involuntarily, like a traitor. Vera struggled with a knife and fork, until she discovered she was quite enjoying her meal with her fingers. Anonymous fatuously dropped a knife which landed with a loud clatter on the floor. All eyes were upon him. Instantly he withdrew, stuck his body rigidly against the wall, with his palms resting flat on the table. He noticed that his fingers were growing fat. "But this is just beside the point," he addressed the unwaning stares, as if continuing an argument which the others did not know about and which had begun with the history of his country; "this is just beside the point. The people that I represent, that constitute me, aren't at all Papuans. We aren't real." "We may not be real," said Vera, calmly, "but we are Papuans living and thinking outside ourselves." "And that's Papua New Guinean?" put in Sheila with a stare of disgust. "Of course, of course," Vera spoke hastily, returning the other's stare of disgust; "and who would want to be as limited as your Papua New Guinean sentiment?" "Thieves. Psycho-murderers," came the voices of the *kung fu* children from outside. Anonymous got up from his chair, filled his glass to the brim with Sheila's white wine but, before walking out to the back verandah to watch the children with it, emptied the glass in a single gulp. *I live in self-delusions, so am I accused. My life, full of fantasies and visions of internal sublimations, deathly Saturday night boozings and mourning Sunday ring-for-records, silently repeats a child's universal question: 'Mama, yumi go we nau?' On my calm pool of innocent desires of not-to-be pained liberties, systematic ripples of injustice drown my floating soul. Indifferently I walk on, no longer heeding a Samaritan's faint echoes 'Hey! Stop! Stop! How can you be the one and only victim in this big wide free world?' Yet in my 'introversions' – olsem through the eyes of vampires and nocturnal hallucinations, laka? – I recognise me, the lusman, in the mirror of your own illusions; the world you imitate, wantok, absents you and me."*

Dead fire. Thick jungle in darkness. A river flooding in the night. Flying foxes flap around breadfruit trees; wings get soaked. The flying dogs fall to the earth, bottoms first. Cold rain drumming a lullaby on each sago thatched roofs. *Karude!* A village lies in sleep. A child cuddles himself up in the warmth of its mother. And dreams of peace for the villagers, away from the nightmares of the city. Tomorrow the sun will come again. The jungle will wake. Trees will turn green through light mists; sunlight against tall wood, dancing lianas, lawyer canes. The birds will sing. So flow on Gira, Gira of the Binandere country, through the night, down to the mouth of dawn, to the wide sea of my internal expansion. Only in the mind. Fingers move again. Feeling. Thinking. It's snowing! At 80°F in Moresby. Squalid natives stand, clapping and cheering like on Palm Sunday, rejoicing upon the arrival of ashened polar bears clad in ice cubes; black polar bears the elders are, they stroll on amid the cheering, bearing keys to some complacent doors. It will take years for those squalid natives to grow up to see flowers bloom from a genius of car wrecks. Today banana trees grow on Hubert Murray Highway, their leaves of aluminium, bearing in abundance fruits of polluted tyres, all in a longing to lift the cloud of our dismay; our rain of hope lies buried in the villages to where the native sons resort. Marketeers sit under fuming iron roofs, dreaming of gutters to drip coins for their pumpkin tops, on the days we flee the office to revive sanity through our crimes of going on leave without pay. Our redemption from the present dread means libelled-to-coffin *kanumida* that silently float from your village to mine, your island to mine, your land to mine, through your recent popular records and my ancient *kundu* vibrations, and here are we together, at last, as one, and in desperate reach of the hands for the embracing presence of each other's absence. Then, and only then, I felt you were here and I there with you, when I read my favourite poet again and again and saw your face and when you played your most solitary records over and over and remembered we have never met. *Tasol*, these are our hasty decisions from their premature suspicions that ill-define our presence, while somewhere in this city's suburbs one of us dies of loneliness. The barren saints lock themselves in –

scared by our silent deaths of innocence – and the sun no longer glares upon the frozen keys to our acquaintance. From a midday sun we are but dawn and dusk at once, allowing *olhaus meri* and madmen pilot this ship as we marvel, *'Ogi! Dam, da mebo? Da mebo?'* with our past shrugging, *"Na gae, na gae..."*. There is no voice for us to cry or laugh, *tasol i orait* – we are useless gods carrying buckets of shanty dung without morning *kai,* lunch, *na* sunset *kai. Wantok, ating Tumbuna blo yu mi idai pinis* with the fire; left us not even a fate, and frozen in a north/ south pole of an unmelting reality. Outside this, and this only, Jimi Damebo could hear the familiar living sounds. Water trickling. Firewood being chopped. Morning sounds. He felt at ease.

"What are you doing running after women for?" 'I'm not, I'm not," answered Nathaniel's companion, the New Ireland youth; "she owes us an explanation." They were chasing after Miss Jennifer Stork who had easily rounded a corner with her long legs and disappeared. When they rounded the corner they saw a familiar Datsun driving off. "What about the other judges?" asked Nathaniel. "They can't be located. As usual." Cars whizzed past them as they were waiting to cross the road, to the milk bar, then walk down from it. Horns blared, startling ailing souls in the serenity of human ribs and chest muscles. When at last they were on the other side they turned in time to see a bus drive past, tightly packed with the 4:06 pm-rush crowd. A young woman's head popped out through a window of the bus and screamed, "Nathaniel." He waved; *"Ewa."* "That's the girl you brought to the Fellowship last Saturday," said his companion; "What's wrong with her? Thought I saw her crying." "Vera doesn't cry." They walked down the city's main street, waited for the cars to clear the crossing, then resumed their walk down to the Bottom Pub and Steamies. At the Bottom Pub they waved to some *wantoks* but being as usually 'broke' as they were, they strolled on, round the corner, to Steamies, to the music shop. At the music shop they wanted to do some sight-shopping but the lady had kindly advised them that she was 'closing'. "Don't you think it's unfair," Peter, the New Irelander, was complaining; "I thought they wanted original music, orginal songs. Not derivations like 'Amazing Grace'. They are mad." "No, they aren't, my *wantok,*" said Nathaniel bitterly. "The judges were right; you lost the contest. You always lose – win or lose – you lose." Earlier during the day at work, that Monday, Nathaniel and his companion had received a phone call from the leader of the Fellowship announcing that the winner of the song and music contest was a group from a nearby village with their song 'Amazing Grace'. "It was heart-warming," the judges were quoted through the phone by the leader, "it was original, and it expressed the common interest, sentiment and concern of the people." "I see," Peter, who had answered the phone, said; "I see. I see," and he thought, "It's good to encourage the villagers like that, but don't you think it's murder?" He then recalled that on the printed sheets of the competition's rules were the directions; "Entries must be original music or songs, must reflect the sentiment of the people, and must express the Christian interests of Papuans and New Guineans". The note added: "The judges' decision will be final". Then the leader of the Fellowship had concluded: "Although you and Nathaniel almost won the fourth prize, both of you deserve commendation. The results of the contest will appear in the *Post Courier* tomorrow. Thank you very much for your effort; and please don't stop singing." "I'm fed up; fed up," said Nathaniel as they were waiting to cross the road again. To the crowd that passed them, he yelled "I'm fed up with belonging to a group for nothing. I'm fed up with halfeducated, underdeveloped, dishonest judges. You all are immorally inhuman and incomplete. Fucking uncivilised savages." They crossed the road and decided to walk along the seawall, "because last time I walked that top road a stupid dog bit me on the shin". Peter said nothing. He tucked his hands firmly in his hip pockets and watched the concrete passing beneath him. Abruptly Nathy turned to his companion: "I'm sorry, I'm sorry, *tambu.* "Why?" the other responded, quietly. "Well, I'm sorry for being tough on you when all we deserved was a loss like this." Peter looked up; smiled. "It's as horrible as falling in love with a girl one night just to learn the next day that she's engaged to someone else." He was still smiling. But in his eyes, slightly crimsoned by seventeen years of silent existence, under that seventeen year-old calm smile, Nathaniel, at twenty-two, noticed signs of maturity, endurance, persistence. "He's a good Christian," thought Nathaniel, and they strolled on. At Newtown Hostel, before parting for their own rooms to change, Nathaniel asked, "Hey tambu, did you say Vera was crying?" "Who's Vera?" asked Peter. "You know, the one you saw in the bus." "Oh. Well, I thought I saw her crying, and she looked as if – as if she was screaming for help." "Thanks," said Nathy, and thought, she probably felt lonely; that happens, after a day's work in the office. He then remembered that during the day at their Department he had received a circular advising him not to use the phone for "personal interests". Only the top boys have such privileges; no wonder they don't trust each other. He ran up to the Warden of Hostels and asked for the master key; he ran down with it and opened Room No. 13. A gentle gust of wind entered the room with him; loose papers fluttered about but helplessly fell flat on the unswept floor in a way friendly dogs wag their tails and rise to their heels but settle again after encountering strangers. He collected them all and placed them in a fresh folder. He collected the rest of the folders and neatly piled them on the desk. The door slammed shut by itself and Nathaniel started; a near-musky smell, almost like that of a human corpse, rose to his nose. He felt uneasy. He hurriedly collected the 'Random Notes', the books from the shelf and placed them on top of the folders. A folder, which lay open and revealing foolscaps of handwriting, caught his eyes from under the desk. He bent down and picked it up.

> hello
> what is your
> I see you in the bus every morning
> you stare me I stare you
> then we part
> sister/brother
> if only I could know
> your address?

"It's no use," thought Nathaniel, shutting the folder. "It's no use listening to—a dead man? Was Vera crying? Why hasn't Sheila rung? Probably later. In the Mess. Might as well ring myself and find out. No; he had fallen into a hole. He had no ten toea coins for the phone in the Mess. The Warden of the hostels too complained of telephone bills. "But this is important," Nathaniel battled with his conscience. "A man's dying. Got to find out how he is. Got to –. We understand your concern, Mr Nathaniel Tabonaboni. Perfectly. But give us time; give us time. We will look into the matter, don't you worry yourself to death. Next week, when we have paid off last month's telephone bills. Okay?" Nathaniel opened the cupboard which acted as a wardrobe. He found two pairs of faded blue jeans, three dyed purple T-shirts, four working shirts and shorts, some socks and a pair of Hush Puppies. He brought them all out and placed them in the middle of the room. Above the cupboard was a brown leather suitcase, already adorned with dust and cobwebs. He brought it down and packed the clothes in it. Then he found a transistor radio on the shelf just above the head of the bed. He tested it. The batteries were working. He tuned in to Radio Northern Province.

Aia Mamo ga nasa
duobo-vevera tambove

He switched it off. He looked around the room. Nothing else left; only the near-musky smell and the silence of James St. Nativeson's absence. On the empty desk, however, he saw an empty marmalade bottle. The bottle, with its lid tightly secured, formed a vacuum for itself. In the vacuum, Nathaniel found a heart-shaped copper beating with Vera's initials on one side and Jimi's on the other. He closed the lid again and placed the bottle in the suitcase, after which he locked it. He locked the door to Room No. 13 and carried the suitcase down to his room. The suitcase was heavy. Like a coffin. Nathaniel had his shower and rejoined Peter in the latter's room. They walked down to the Mess and sat a table away from the rest of the clerks. Sheila didn't ring. "You look upset," said Peter. "I'm okay." After dinner they walked back to the hostels and went to Nathaniel's room to listen to the radio.

'To love music is to feel you have a soul'. Who said that? Vera's mind wandered back to her brief lodging at the University where she had done her first year. She read it in a short story tentatively written by an Anuki student some years ago. "Well, I sing because I believe that to love music is to feel you have a soul". Her Chemistry lecturer informed Vera that the writer was disillusioned; that he forgot reality; he had no licence to write – whatever that was, and well, he was such a child, trying to sound intelligent at the age of nineteen. 'Look, it is not wise believing in this writer; it just isn't safe.' What they, the Papuans and New Guineans should write about, continued the lecturer with the experiment – and Vera noted, or thought she had, that the lecturer was holding an empty test tube over the buns en burner; her fear had been that, out of sheer exhaustion of its own emptiness with the exception of a few foreign gases which only the experts could identify, the bloody glass might have cracked any moment – were stories that helped shape and developed the nation; a writer's duty is to provide national consciousness, to stimulate national unity; to educate the village masses; to guide those promising young writers who are lost to come back to the right path of creative writing; to go through the right kind of training and ultimately take over from their expatriate counterparts as the future literary leaders of this country; to make one plus one equal two and not five or ten, no, not even x; to – to –. Vera passed the other subjects, after which she left the University. The Chemistry lecturer wrote her a letter advising her to submit the most important assignments of the course. She wrote back giving the lecturer her permission to fail her. She applied for an arts fellowship in Australia. "Not that I am betraying my country; not that I am a traitor; nor am I applying to represent my country in any way whatsoever. I just want to become a writer, along with those other free writers of the world. And we do not intend to promote anger. I repeat: we do not intend to promote anger. Let the black man's critical art kill itself with its own black vomit." Music. It revived her senses after the day's work in the office. She was alive again, heaving a deep sigh of resilience, omitting from her mind the memory of her Chemistry lecturer. "Stiff dialogue," thought Vera of that particular lecturer;

blind encouragement without the legal securities. A gentleman, quite possibly another clerk and wearing a modest pot-belly, rose from his seat for her to sit down. Vera did so. With a blank smile; "If they are as kind as all this they are unsuccessful heterosexuals." The bus was packed; sweaty stench of humanity infatuated her nostrils. Those that were standing, sardined and hanging onto the rails like labourers travelling to rural plantations, had hardly room to move, to breathe. A girl standing not far from Vera , her hands vertically raised for the rails, was struggling to at least move a fraction of an inch to be free of an old man who also stood in similar pose, their noses touching. She winced and complained in Motu. A young clerk, standing just behind the pot-bellied *lusman,* was slowly, slowly dozing off. Vera noticed that he was nursing a brown parcel which looked as if it contained a bacardi bottle. She gazed at him lazily until the young clerk, at an unexpected jerk of the bus, dropped the parcel. The bottle broke, the parcel tore, pieces of glass scattered all around the spot of disturbance, and a syrupy fluid escaped in all directions. Bare feet and shoes were instinctively uplifted, to be free of the broken glass pieces. A piece landed between Vera's feet and she bent down to study it. "Mothers", the broken piece of glass seemed to tell Vera, "this is important: as your child grows in this world, he needs vitamin C, every day." The syrupy fluid flowed on, reluctantly, wasted, and a few shoes carefully swept the broken glass towards the space under the seats where no one would dare tread. The bare feet and shoes were again planted on the floor of the bus, and the vitamin C was downtrodden. The young clerk or father shut his eyes, opened them, and blinked two or three times until the pupils became red and his vision blurred. "Is his baby boy or girl?" someone asked. An overweight woman sitting at the left of Vera laughed uncontrollably until she was breathless. The music from the bus made Vera forget the other passengers, their smells, their remarks and gentle protests. It gave life to the content of her easy-heaving chest. She was climbing to the top of a cliff with a rope; James was holding the other end from the top. She called up to him to pull, and he responded with a smile; he was pulling up her soul – "Ah, stop the fucken music, driver," the clerk before her yelled. The rope broke and Vera fell headlong into the rocky cliff below. She died with the music. The bus stopped at the hospital. She left her dead body in the bus and walked out. *Wanpis*. A few boys whistled to her; she waved to them, but walked up to a bearded Australian just coming out of the main gate. *"Oro da, nambori,"* she greeted him. *"Oro da. Oro da,"* the nambori returned her the greeting; "been trying to contact you lately. Look at you, just look at you. Where've you been hiding yourself? Where are you hiding? Where are you hiding?" "I don't," she said. "You must come up to the house for some time then." "I must, I must," she said and smiled. Then in an unexpected outburst the Australian yapped, *"God na wantok i toe, na nambori i toe, kokoatu nato i toe, na nasi i toe, na - na - "* *"Na dubo-vevera ena,"* Vera helped him out with the language. They both laughed: *"Aia Godi."* "Now," he then said, "let me see, oh yes, you've forgotten our phone number again. Mmm, naughty, naughty..." Guilty, Vera looked at her toes playing indifferently on her brown leather sandals. "Yes, yes," the Australian was mumbling while pulling out a small pad and a pen from his breast pocket, "like the rest of your mob you forget your *wantoks* and *tambus*. Here," he gave her the phone number; "I don't suppose you approve of us *lusman* much, but Lucy and the kids are missing you a lot, Vera. You must come up and see them." She looked up. "I must, I must," she said, but all emotion seemed to have escaped her. "Ah, you still won't come up," the Australian said, feeling rejected, severed. "No, it's not that, *koatu naka,"* she said; "I – ." She averted her eyes. She was anxious to go away; "I – I'm looking for the place where the most injured patients are." "That must be, let me see now – Ward 7 it is. Straight ahead, and first floor up the stairs. And don't forget to give us a ring, will yer?" She waved without looking back. It was cool in the ward. She was afraid she might be walking through a cemetery. Two or three nurses in blue stealthily trod the polished floors, from room to room. She walked past a room where four junior nurses were having a conference; possibly having a yarn about a certain boy one of them saw somewhere. She held up a nurse who was looking busy over a sheet of notes. She asked her about James. "Oh," said the nurse, but instantly appeared contrite.

"This one isn't educated enough," thought Vera. Then the nurse said, "Come with me, please." It was a return journey for Vera; they found themselves outside. They walked through the car park and turned left. The nurse pointed to a green building far up the road, and said nothing. When Vera hesitated with silent enquiry, the nurse insisted on pointing to the green building without words. "Thanks," said Vera and walked on. Three elderly men, the villagers to the city, walked silently after her. She saw a group of people gathered infront of the green building. Some women in the group were quietly shedding tears. "Oh," said Vera and abruptly stood still. Time, red Moresby earth, green trees, buildings and the blue sky, all spun: she was the axis of that ferris-wheel.

> hungry vultures circled
> a clear spinning fireball of blue
> illusive to the reverieminded
> an existing azure of inexistence
> eerily clanging and twanging
> a mystic tune of silent din

One of the elders behind Vera quietly said, 'The women weep for the dead." And another responded in the same tone, 'That is the place where they reclaim their fated relatives." The third intoned, "In the village we hear of it all on the radio. Here we see for ourselves with our own eyes." The three villagers overtook her and walked on, their heads bowed. Vera did a sudden about-turn and saw the bitumen road before her through a shower curtain. She bolted, without stopping, through the rain, thunder, fog and mist of her own sorrow, her suffering, until she entered the telephone room of her hostel. She fumbled through her pockets, found a ten toea piece, inserted the coin and dialled a number. When she heard Sheila's husband's voice, she shrieked and swore, calling him all the names she could think of, and promising him that she would kill herself, until a thick black cloud smothered her consciousness.

"'The rate of suicide in the Northern Province is fairly high.' Was it you who told me that, dear? Or somebody else?" Sheila did not answer her husband. She was quietly sipping her cold tea at the table. She had a hard day at work; she was tired, weak and her mind could not keep up with her husband's. He waited for an answer from her, until he was bored with waiting. He went to the bedroom and wore his orange working shirt. He came out, kissed her on the perspiring forehead and opened the door to the front verandah. "I'm going out for half-an-hour. Don't bother preparing the dinner. I'll get myself something to eat when I return." She said nothing. He walked out. He circled the house and found himself in the back street. Even dusk is bored this evening; it is burnt sienna all of a sudden. But when he looked up again a moment later the west side of the sky offered him a wilderness of Mekeo rice, ready for harvest. In the street the *kung fu* children confronted him. He played along with them in the dust until he was free of them. "Thief! Psychomurderer." He felt the weight of someone else's guilt upon his shoulders again. He caught a bus to Boroko, alighted and strolled through the late evening air to Vera's hostel. "You must hurry, my brother," said a girl who knew him; "I will close the gates in fifteen minutes." "Thanks, Vivianne," he said, as she let him through. He found three girls in Vera's room, all councelling her. She was lying on her back on the bed. The three girls made as if to excuse themselves from the room but he raised a hand; "No, no, don't mind me, sisters. Just finish what you are doing." But the girls insisted on leaving both of them alone. He sat down at the edge of the bed. "You went there on your own," he said, sounding apologetic. "I almost killed myself," she said; "but – ." As usual with Vera, she forgot to add anything else. "What stopped you?" he knocked at the door of her reticence. "Got to finish that play first, you bastard." "Oh." "And anyway," she added, turning her head away, "thanks for coming – doctor." "Sheila's upset too," he said, not minding the sarcasm; "said nothing to me, all afternoon today." "I'm afraid of your wife," she said; "I'm afraid of broad daylight darkness." Tears came to her eyes. He reached out a hand for her's but, remembering he was married, withdrew it. "Hell, did you notice I'm all on my own now," she wept in between four-letter words. "Endure, endure," he told himself and the floor beneath him. Then to Vera he said, "One day you'll resolve yourself." "Thanks, Father," she retorted; "but I'm all alone. Alone, do you hear?" "But that's beside the point, Vera," he said painfully; "that's just beside the point." "You are always beside the point," she said aloud; "with all your cheating, your lies. Cold blooded, half-educated traitor." She almost spat at him. She sat up; she tried to push him away, but he held her hand firmly. "Let go of me," she said calmly, and he released her. He stood up, dug his hands in his hip pocket and began pacing the little room, like Archiebald Goldsworth. Then remembering, he picked up Vera's little bag from the desk, took out a packet of cigarettes and offered her one. He took out one for himself, lit hers and his, then resumed pacing the floor. "I must be going now," he said, thinking, "she'sright; I've betrayed her." "Those names I called you this afternoon," Vera said, "I think you deserve them all." He looked at her and grinned. "Thanks," he then said, "but I think it is about time you started calling me the dedicated, intellectual bourgeois pig." He shrugged; "I've no choice. Can't flee the city; can't abandon myself. As old Jimi Damebo once put it, 'Who shall greet us then, we who flee the city to the jungle of our silence that hangs on a thin thread, so fragile, as it is here and where also four *dobucorners* so solid, bar Civilisation?' Ha. What frail pre-emptions. Nope. Can't abandon myself. Having a wife and family is no excuse, I know; but one day in the life of a man there is this"—he shrugged again – "this business of belonging, a moment of decision, a desire to battle it all out, until he discovers that he is not totally alone. No, not even being just the fatherless native." "The dedicated, intellectual bourgeois pig," Vera was testing the words through a careless laugh; she was grinding the tooth of a new spear. Then, ready to hurl the spear at him, she said, "Who will applaud you? You are just a sperm. A random sperm, squirted with the seminal flood from a white *lusman*, which trickled along the white walls, down to the relieving embrace of Enita, of the earth. Ha. You were lucky, friend." The sharp spear pierced him, and he knew he would never live again. He shut his eyes, numb.When he re-opened them, Vera threw her cigarette butt at his feet and whispered, "Bastard." This time she meant the word. "What about your fellowship thing?" he asked with a sigh, a sigh which he wanted to use to cure his wound. She pointed to three envelopes on the desk. He picked them up and read them all. A smile swept across his face, massaging his wounded insides. "For three months?" he asked. "They might want me to stay longer," she answered and looked at the floor. He extended a congratulatory hand; she took it. Her hand was lifeless. "What I want," she then looked up to him and said, "is to go away from this place. Go altogether."

"Did anyone tell you I'm a good radio technician?" asked Peter. "Most New Irelanders aren't but you are the first one to tell me that," replied Nathaniel. Nathaniel sat on his bed, watching his companion at work on the floor. Peter had taken St Nativeson's transistor radio to pieces with a screw driver, although there was nothing wrong with it, and was having difficulty in re-wiring the electrical chords. He had previously done that a lot of times with the other clerks' radio sets, and had even won a reputation for himself. One day, a Notherner brought him a set which he had claimed was not functioning well. "Oh but *nambori,*" Peter had protested then, "you know I cannot possibly fix this." "Why not?" asked the other. "Because it's already buggered," Peter had said, helplessly. Now he was playing around with St Nativeson's set because it wasn't 'buggered'. "May I offer you a professional statement that you are at serious technical fault?" Nathaniel said with a laugh. But Peter had succeeded with his re-wiring and, as if complimenting him, a voice from the transistor said, 'And now the news in detail...' "I've done it, I've done it," yelled Peter, and he was hopping around the room. "Shoosh," said Nathaniel, and they jumped onto the floor, huddled round the transistor, their mouths wide open with shock and incredulity. "'A man has died from serious head injuries at the Port Moresby General Hospital this morning. He was JimiDamebo, twenty-three years old, of Karude Village in the IomaSub-Province of the Northern Province. A police spokesman said today that Jimi Damebo had been rushed by a crowed of fifteen to twenty men armed with beer bottles, iron bars and hard timber who battered his head to unconsciousness, during the labourer's uprising last Saturday. The spokesman for the doctors said that Jimi Damebo had been fighting hard for his life since that time until his death at six o'clock this morning. Jimi Damebo was employed as a Clerk by the Department of – .' The wiring with Peter's skill snapped and the two of them darted for the radio in another clerk's room for better reception. 'The Secretary of the Archiebald Goldsworth Community Welfare Fund, Mrs Sheila Willborough, said this afternoon that the Community has donated four hundred kina for the body of Jimi Damebo to be flown to Ioma on Friday. Mrs Willborough has withdrawn from providing newsreporters with further details. This news comes to you –." Nathaniel and Peter stole out of their clerical acquaintance's room without a word. Silence hung over the air of Newtown Hostel; a few clerks could be heard murmuring. But a lot whispered a name well known to them; it was whispered from room to room as Nathaniel and Peter walked past. The night, the warm air, the trees: the dark earth and the gentle wind too, all whispered, echoed and re-echoed the name. It was just a name, an ordinary traditional name, that was being mentioned, quietly. At the door just before Nathaniel's room a little Northerner rushed out crying, "Carelessness, that's what I call it. Sheer stupidity and carelessness." And the clerk was blurting out the words through torrents of tears. The Christians at the Hostel, including free-Jesus believers like Nathaniel and Peter, assumed the death of Jimi Damebo as their's also, their second spiritual death in the Hostel's history. Tomorrow, perhaps, they would wake up fresh with the sun. But they would all be walking corpses then, Nathaniel concluded; and this was the new destiny that befell them, in a country whose people were too frightened to admit, even within themselves, that they had yet to embrace human *raison d'etre,* in a country where a child was given a water pistol without the preconvictions of where and to whom it will point to press the trigger, in a country where there were no wars, no political terrorism, no executions nor military torture, let alone have her men just stare a brother to a raw, moral death.

They had each applied for a day's leave without pay, for that Friday. Peter came with them, substituting James St. Nativeson. Anonymous, after much painful effort, seeing that he was barely twenty-three and the company could only welcome customers twenty-five years old or older, had succeeded in renting a car for them. His pleadings were at last heeded and he signed his nonexistent parents' names. The lady at the counter was kind: "Now you just take good care of the car, lover, because you know how much it will cost you if you wreck it." To the lady, who was then studying the cards with her customers' names, Abel Willborough was another happy, multiracial, society name. The others were glumly waiting for him near the cars. "Which one?" Nathaniel called. Sheila's husband ran back to the lady's office; she came out with him to the door and pointed to a creamy white Datsun. But he was disappointed to discover later that the car had no radio. In the car were Peter, Nathaniel and Vera. Anonymous drove them to the airport. Outside the Liklik Air office a little crowd gathered, most of them writers and students from the University. Sheila had worked harder than the rest in that she saw to the removal of the corpse from the mortuary to the airport; she had sent a telegram each to the Office-in-Charge of the Ioma Patrol Post and the parents of Jimi Damebo two days previously, and was now silently watching with the crowd the coffin being wheeled to a light aircraft. The others walked up and joined her. She motioned her husband to come and stand near her. They said nothing to each other. A newsreporter pleasantly approached Sheila but she waved him away. "Careful there," an Australian called to the men who were pushing the coffin; "that's your nation's destiny." Tiredness and fatigue overcame Sheila; she dropped back into her husband's arms with short jerks of inevitable sobs: *"Auweu wee,alou alou* – what have I done? What have I done?" He squeezed her flesh reassuringly. An African among the crowd walked over to Sheila and her husband and made as if to ask a few questions, but Anonymous said, "You must forgive me, Doctor. She feels faint." The African walked away, looking disturbed but thoughtful. Anonymous carried Sheila to the car, placed her gently at the back seat and watched from there. Vera was clawing at the fence, sobbing vigorously and repeatedly calling out James' names. Peter and Nathaniel just stood beside her and watched the coffin. Father Jefferson's absence could be excused since he was living away from Port Moresby; but Mr. Archiebald Goldsworth was not there, which could mean that he was too busy to come and offer words of condolence, although Anonymous imagined this was an occurrence purely left to the philosophy of self-reliance. The African Doctor was now engaged in a deep conversation with the newsreporter who was busily scribbling away on his note pad. Then doors were heard being slammed from the direction of the light aircraft. Vera screamed and as Peter and Nathy caught her from falling, the aircraft taxied out to the main runway. Minutes later it was airborne, resounding its own roar of independence: one breathing pilot, a dead poet and the sky of serenity, anonymity.

In the Binandere tradition, as much as in any other, whenever there is death there is a time for mourning and a time for rejoicing. The earth, the virgin jungle, the rivers and the blue sky, follow that tradition. And the taro also respond: a wife walks through the garden with a b*ilum* slung over her head and in seeing her the taro mourn, they exchange inquisitive stares amongst themselves, and ultimately weep out the question, 'Sisters, brothers, who is it among us that must be pulled out today?' The question echoes down the multitude of taro, and the wind re-echoes the question. Yet there comes a day when the husband walks through the garden: the taro rejoice, they dance and wave their leaves joyously even though the air is as still as can be, knowing that it is the father, the man of the soil, who has returned to visit them. In the village there is eating and drinking, there is singing and dancing, which marks the end of sorrow and the beginning of happiness. Anonymous had never been to that part of the country, although through his wife who had spent her childhood there, and through Vera and Jimi Damebo who were Binandere, he had come to recognize the sacred essence of that legend of taro. Armed with this knowledge he drove his friends straight to the Waigani Market. There he bought some taro, a portion of smoked

wallaby and some *orabu* and pumpkin tops. The others joined
him with the preparation of the feast; Peter and Nathaniel had
each bought a carton of beer; Vera had assumed Sheila's duties
of buying *dim dim* food from the Supermarket and Sheila just sat
in the car and watched her friends. A smile swept across her face.
They were alive again. They were the new people. The profound
breed, reborn. Instantly she jumped out of the car, ran into the
bottle shop and re-appeared a few minutes later with a large bottle
of red wine. The others laughed and she no longer felt guilty.
Nathaniel and Peter persuaded Anonymous to drive them to the
Hostel to pick up their guitars and James St Nativeson's suitcase.
The afternoon found them at the house of Sheila and husband and
they were all smiles again. They feasted and Peter and Nathaniel
sang songs derived from the poetry of Jimi Damebo. In the middle
of the feast Anonymous switched on the radio and they all listened
attentively to the news." A crowd of writers, University students
and a few members of the academic staff gathered outside the
Liklik Air office at eleven o'clock this morning to see the body of
Mr Jimi Damebo flown to Ioma, Northern Province. The body of
Mr Damebo will be received by the parents and relatives and will
be buried in his home village. Those in the crowd have expressed
their deepest regret for the untimely death and premature loss of
Mr Jimi Damebo whom a senior student has described as 'the
nation's outspoken poet and artist'. However, that is not all. The
visiting lecturer of Law to the University of Papua New Guinea,
Doctor Aiya Awod Obala, being among the crowd of writers and
University students, is reported to have curtly remarked, '"This
is a serious matter ever to come out of the Third World Black
countries, which deserves careful scrutiny, in particular Mrs
Willborough's exclamation, *'Auweu wee, alou, alou –* what have
I done? What have I done?'" Doctor Awod Obala went on to say
that the meaning of Mrs Willborough's exclamation required
serious academic observation. Mrs Willborough, the Secretary of
the Archiebald Goldsworth Community Welfare Fund, has again
withdrawn from providing our newsreporter with any information.
That's the end nf the news. The next news from this station will
be –." Anonymous switched the transistor off; now here we have

a country on trial. "Did you hear that, Sheila?" Nathaniel quietly asked. They all eyed her, but not through accusing stares. Nathaniel walked over to Mrs Willborough and, placing a reassuring hand on her shoulder, said, "You have done all that could have been done, sister. And who wouldn't dare?" Peter, almost with a bow, said, "We have not lost hope in you, sister. " "Thanks," said Sheila and threw an uncertain glance at her husband. Then she watched his fingers. The fingers weren't moving. She threw another glance at his face. He nodded. With a smile. Then Anonymous felt the absence of Vera; he found the real Vera out on the back verandah, gazing mutely to the west. "You are not drinking," he pretended to be alarmed. Vera smiled. *"Pom gurina,"* she said, and he was surprised to hear her speak Enita's tongue; "we have a long weekend of feasting, my brother." Inside they heard Nathaniel say, *"Ewa, awelupoa ma amaka hougana i nae, bo?"* Vera answered, *"Na ge i tae."* Anonymous said nothing. Above them a jet plane whistled by, forming a southward arc and leaving a trace of black which stained the reddish sky. "One of these days," he thought, at dusk like this, she will fly away." He watched the dusk with Vera: she was calm and silent; everything had now come to a standstill; no more trees being chopped down; no more thoughts of the past, nor letters of Save-Our-Souls to the ecclesiastical All Saints'. He breathed in, breathed out, and breathed in again, absorbing dusk. He turned to Vera, almost blocking her vision. "You don't approve of dusks much, do you, Abel?" Vera then asked, after noting a certain mystery in his eyes. "Of course I do," he answered nevertheless, with a smile; "in fact, without a single dusk of a day in my life I would never feel complete."

He could now easily apply a happy look on his own face.